*'Sardinia is a place lost between Europe
and Africa and belonging to nowhere...'*

D.H. LAWRENCE

BITTER HONEY

RECIPES AND STORIES FROM THE ISLAND OF SARDINIA

photography by
MATT RUSSELL

LETITIA CLARK

Hardie Grant
BOOKS

After God created the earth, he threw the leftover pieces into the Mediterranean Sea. He selected all of the best parts of his creation and placed them upon one of these rocks. This rock he named Sardinia.

SARDINIAN LEGEND

After surveying his work, God realised he had created something too beautiful. There was an imbalance between the beauty of Sardinia and all of the other regions around it. God thought hard about how to redress this balance. And then, he had an epiphany. He created the Sardinians.

SARDINIAN JOKE

It is fair to say that when I began to write this book, I had no idea what I was doing. I was nervous of writing about a culture and a cuisine that was not my own. After worrying quietly about it, I spoke to my boyfriend, Luca:

'I don't care what you are scared of Letiiizzzia', he purred in his Sardinian drawl, 'I care about the food of Sardinia, and I want people to know about it. And anyway' – he added with a grin – 'now I tell all people you are writing it, and everybody want to know you and to give you 'elp and recipes, to show you things and tell you stories, and you 'ere moaning. Ehhh Letiiiiizzzia, it's not just about you!'

In his characteristically frank style, he reminded me of the potential of this book, and the power of recipe books in general. Recipe books are not just books of recipes. They are also chronicles of traditions, stories and memories. They give us insight into people's lives, into their habits and their histories. Food is never just food. It is a memory, a moment recaptured in a mouthful. It is friendship, it is love, it is celebration. Often in the modern world of food, it is easy to lose sight of this. In Sardinia, it is not.

I am not Sardinian. This book does not pretend to be a comprehensive guide to the authentic cuisine of Sardinia. Authenticity is a slippery concept, as anyone who writes about food (especially Italian food) will know. Every cook in Sardinia has their own way of doing things, and to them this is the only way. The Sardinian (and Italian) pride for their regional cuisine is in part what makes it so appealing, but the pursuit of 'authenticity' in recipe writing is often a futile affair. Recipes, like any story, memory or history, are a medley of influences, consequences, necessities and innovations. I was reminded of this recently when Franca – Luca's mother – described 'a traditional Sardinian soup' recipe which was in fact, without a shadow of a doubt, French onion soup.

When I arrived in Sardinia, I realised many things; about myself, about eating, about cooking. Far too trite to say I found myself – and I didn't anyway – but I found my food, and that's a pretty good place to start. Before I came here, I'd worked in restaurants as a professional chef (though I was never very professional) and lived a gypsy-like existence. Drifting from place to place, from job to job. I'd cooked 'Modern British' in a trendy Hackney bistro, I'd worked in a Middle Eastern restaurant and grilled enough spiced lamb chops to last me a lifetime. I'd trained at a well-regarded, French-influenced cookery school. I travelled, tasted and tried relentlessly, and I relished each new recipe, each new cuisine.

What I found myself craving most after all this, however, was simplicity. I was tired of trends, of techniques, of turnips cut into triangles. I wanted to eat and to cook good, simple food. I wanted food that was inherently delicious, but didn't take itself too seriously.

Ultimately, I realised, I wanted to cook home-food, not restaurant-food. Food that didn't try to challenge or to transgress. I wanted to find a cuisine that was so rooted in its – for want of a better word – roots, that no passing fad or fancy could shake its foundations, or sabotage its simplicity. I wanted integrity. I wanted cheese. I wanted wine – 'made in home' as Luca would say – served from plastic petrol containers, and olive oil in old Coke bottles that glowed green and flowed as freely as water. I wanted vegetables that tasted of themselves and didn't need cutting into cubes, or batons or any other arbitrarily abstract shape. I wanted to get to the jagged core of cooking. I wanted Nonna in her slippers shouting at me to grate my own breadcrumbs (I buy breadcrumbs when she's not looking. Sometimes life is too short, and we must all of us choose our battles). I wanted to go back into a home, to the sink and the stove, where it all began.

The glory of Italian food, and the reason why it remains so endlessly popular, is that it is essentially home-cooking. Just like Mamma used to make. It's a crashing cliché, of course, but that doesn't stop it being true. It is interesting that the word *casalinga* (which translates literally as 'housewife') is often used to describe rustic, homemade dishes; recipes that are the favourites of so many, passed down from mother to daughter (or son) over many generations. Marcella Hazan, the doyenne of Italian cooking, puts it far better than me:

> *'(Italian cooking) is cooking for the home kitchen... there is no such thing as Italian* haute cuisine *because there are no high or low roads in Italian cooking. All roads lead to home, to the* cucina di casa, *the only cooking that deserves to be called Italian cooking.'*

Italian cooking is adored worldwide because it is the food of home, and is therefore, ultimately, comfort food. Comfort food is food that makes you either feel at home, or think of home. It doesn't matter where you are, or who's home you happen to be in, it just instils in you that warm, fuzzy, Winnie-the-Pooh feeling that you're somewhere safe, eating something good, and all is not lost. As I said, I'm not Italian – not even close – but somehow, Italian food takes me home.

So how does the food of Sardinia differ, or compare? Sardinian food is a distilled version of Italian food: simpler, more rustic, more wild. The emphasis on tradition and on the importance of eating well is even more pronounced here on this forgotten island. Even more of its ancient delicacies are preserved, even more of its produce grown or made at home.

Sardinia has become my home, and as soon as I moved here, I was reminded that good food is not about being a slave to authenticity, or about complication, technique, or trends, but about sharing, about people and – most importantly – about enjoyment (and also, as you will discover, quite a lot about cheese). The Sardinians I have met have welcomed me into their homes. They have shared their time, their knowledge, their meals and their recipes, with no motive other than their immense love for life, for their land and for their cuisine.

I hope this book will inspire some of that love in your home, too.

Buon Appetito!

A NOTE ON THE PREFACE

Since beginning this book three years ago, many things have changed, most significantly that Luca and I are no longer a couple. He inspired in me the same passion he felt for the food of his home, and for this I will always be grateful. I will think of him whenever I drink a bad espresso, or roast a good chicken.

14th November 2019   *Letitia Clark*

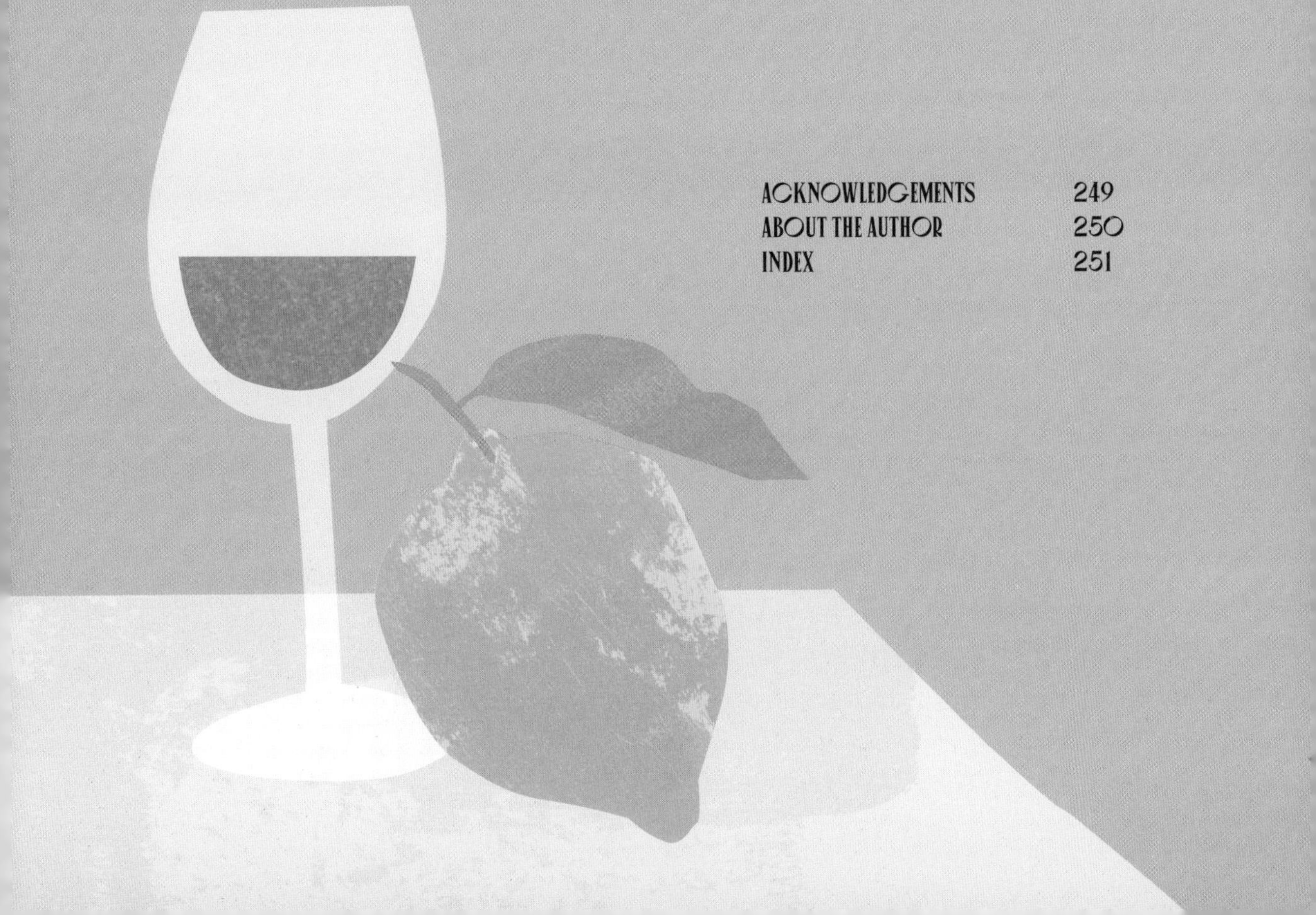

INTRODUCTION

I grew up in Devon in a farmhouse with an orchard full of decrepit apple trees. Autumns were spent picking apples for my father to turn into a lethal cider, or to be boiled into a wobbling amber jelly. I learnt then what I still believe now, that often the best things in life are the simplest – an apple picked from the tree, bread and butter, my mother's béchamel. This is the food that stays with us.

When I arrived in Sardinia, I'd spent the last few years cooking in professional kitchens. I cooked for a living, but I didn't live to cook. Cooking had become something I no longer did for love.

And then, suddenly, a small, round Sardinian popped into my life. We worked together, he on the fryer, me on the grill. He used to feed me crispy fried things when no one was looking. On our first date, he invited me to his home for supper, handed me a glass of wine and a pair of slippers, and proceeded to cook me *pasta al ragù*.

He shuffled around the kitchen in his own *ciabatte*, telling me with inevitable Italian melodrama about the place that was his home, a part of Italy but also a world of its own – Sardinia. He described an island of deliciously simple food, abundant produce and unspoilt countryside, where people lived forever, forgetting to die. An island of 'goats and gangsters!' – my father blustered when I announced my intention of going there. Either way, I was intrigued.

I first visited with Luca in February 2017, for Sa Sartiglia, Oristano's infamous mardi gras festival – a week of medieval horse racing, drinking and eating. The Vacca household was a constant stream of friends, family and passing strangers. The door was open, and everybody was free to wander in. Inside they were welcomed by a table spread with suckling pig, roast lamb, chicken (all from the family farm) ragù, ravioli, bread, olives, wine, fruit and *dolci*. The noise was constant: the TV blaring out live coverage of the race (though it was happening less than 100 metres (300 feet) away, there was too much eating to be done to leave the house) and the excitement was palpable. I drank and ate all day, every day for the whole week. The entire town seemed to pass through during those few days. I was introduced to countless tiny beaming people (Sardinians are famously short, and I am very tall). I kissed more Sardinian cheeks and was bristled by more Sardinian moustaches than I care to remember. Meanwhile Franca, Luca's indomitable mother, would ensure the table was always groaning with food. I marvelled at how she did it all. And then I realised, all the crockery was plastic; the napkins and tablecloths paper. At the end of each epic day of feasting, she would pick the whole lot up in one sweep of her arms and dump it in the bin, then lay the same arrangement for the following day's excesses. The Sardinian way: minimum stress, maximum pleasure.

Carnival over, Luca and I returned home, and to work. A few months later, as we watched Brexit unfold in horror, we made up our minds, packed our bags and left for Sardinia. As soon as I began to research this book, I realised there was enough material to fill at least fifty books. Hundreds of recipes, traditions and stories from a forgotten pocket of the Mediterranean.

A TAVOLA!

To cook like a Sardinian, you have to eat like a Sardinian. Meals here are never a hurried affair. Shops and offices close from 12–4 p.m., as people return home to eat lunch with their families. Weekday lunches easily occupy those four hours, the meal often followed by a *pennichella* (small sleep). Lunches at the weekends or for special occasions, start at midday and finish in the early hours of the next morning.

No snatched sandwiches or lunch 'on the run'; skipping meals is sacrilege. Families always eat together. Whether there is squabbling or silence, it does not matter, Sards are stoical on this point. Food is never merely fuel, it is as significant as love, as sex. And as enjoyable.

POVERI MA BELLI

'Poverty, rather than wealth, gives the good things in life their significance.' — PATIENCE GRAY

Luca's nonna, Giulia, grew up in extreme poverty. Her father, a farm labourer, was ill for most of his life, and her mother had to support the family by making dolci to sell in town. Nonna had to help her mother, and often her father in the fields, walking for up to half a day to and fro. She loves to tell me this story, but like all of her stories, it always ends with a description of her family as *'poveri, ma belli!'*: poor, but beautiful.

Italy's long history of peasant culture means Italian cuisine is often described as *cucina povera* (poor cooking). Sardinian cooking remains true to these principles, following the age-old values of making the most of available ingredients, eating seasonally, salvaging leftovers, using simple and inexpensive foodstuffs such as beans and pulses, and growing as much as possible yourself.

To us in England, it may seem that a cuisine centred around suckling pig, cured hams and salami, fresh fish, olive oil and pecorino is anything but poor. But it is the sparing use of these more expensive items that elevates 'poor' dishes, such as a simple bowl of lentils dressed with strong olive oil or a plate of pasta tossed with pecorino. The raw materials are basic, cheap and easy to procure, which makes it a perfect cuisine for those cooking at home, and on a budget. The luxury items, such as meat and fish, are eaten less frequently, and so are worth spending more money on. Many still rear their own animals and feed them on scraps, so meat costs nothing at all.

The island's rich soil produces an abundance of fruits and vegetables. The pride Sardinians have in this produce is both hilarious and contagious. You can find little here that is not 'the best in the *world!*', as Luca says. Shopping is done almost daily, mostly at markets. Eating seasonally and locally is the only way of life. Nothing is wasted or taken for granted, and cooking is without pretension.

INTRODUCTION

SARDINIA AND THE SARDS

As I got to know the island, it became clear to me that there are two Sardinias: the coast and the interior. The coast is strikingly beautiful, famed for its white beaches and turquoise sea. It is for this that Sardinia is known; for its north coast especially, known as the *Costa Smeralda* (Emerald Coast). A popular holiday destination originally built up and popularised by the business magnate Aga Khan VI in the 1960s, it is now a playground for the rich and famous; a world of superyachts and oligarchs. In startling contrast, the rest of the island is predominantly rural and unspoilt. Here the landscape is almost biblical: vast plains of sheep pasture, sweeping green valleys of olives and vines dotted with Nuragic ruins and hilltop villages. It is possible to drive for hours and the only form of life one will see is a herd of sheep, skinny and roman-nosed, their long ears skirting the ground as they graze, bells tinkling, and a lone sheepdog watching over them nearby. The food here does not seem to have changed much in the last 2,000 years; it is a simple, rustic cuisine for shepherds.

Sardinia is the second largest island in the Mediterranean, situated in the middle of the watery expanse between Italy, Spain and North Africa. Though it became part of Italy under Garibaldi's unification at the end of the 19th century, Sardinia has always set itself a world apart. Sardinian history is a catalogue of invasion and colonisation – by, amongst others, the Romans, the Spanish and the Phoenicians – and whilst the various settlers have left their marks on areas of the coast, the interior is still very much as it always was. Being an island, it has managed to preserve a lot of its original identity (something Sardinians are very proud of), keeping its customs – and its cooking – untouched. Inevitably ingredients and techniques have woven their way into the cuisine over the centuries: spices from the Phoenicians; wine and olive oil from the Romans; a sherry-like wine (Vernaccia) from the Spanish; but overall the Sardinians have managed to retain a fiercely independent culinary identity.

Sards have their own language (*Sardo*) which is the closest language to Latin still in use today; and they have their own way of doing things. They cling limpet-like to these traditions with a tenacity that I find both wonderful and infuriating.

I was once told by a Sardinian that the only reason the Mafia never caught on here, despite numerous attempts to initiate it, was that Sardinians simply weren't interested in partaking in any kind of group activity. Organisations of all kinds are viewed with scepticism by the Sards, and rules often flagrantly ignored.

The Sards may be famously belligerent, stubborn and proud, but above all they are charming and generous. Frank to a fault, they love to laugh at themselves, and at everything else. They often break into patriotic song in the middle of routine conversations, or say with comical solemnity, 'yes yes, but Sardinia is a *paradise*' if another place is mentioned. There even exists a theory (propagated by a Sardinian archaeologist) that Sardinia is the lost city of Atlantis.

Atlantis or not, I cannot deny that there is a certain something about this island. It is a place both mundane and magical. It gets under your skin. As Claudia Roden writes:

'I don't know if it is because Sardinians are unbelievably generous and hospitable and their land is so beautiful, or because their food evokes the simple life or a remote past, or because it is simply so good, but it provokes a strong emotion of the kind you never forget.'

Still very much an island of regions, the region I found myself in was Oristano, the centre-west of the island. One of Sardinia's great medieval cities, Oristano is also just an everyday town. It is a town of peeling paint, cobbled streets and balconies blousy with bougainvillaea. At noon, the piazza is full of men taking *aperitivo*, bald brown heads glinting in the midday sun, each as shiny as a polished nut.

Luca's family have lived here for generations. His great grandfather used to farm saffron in the fields nearby, his grandfather (a wheeler-dealer in the Del Boy mould) made gelato in his kitchen, coloured it with green dye and sold it on the street as Oristano's finest 'pistachio'. Luca's father and his brother still farm rice in the Oristano countryside. A love of food – spiced with what Luca would call 'motherfuckery' – runs deep in the Vacca veins.

SLOW AND SLOWER

Life here is slow.

Sardinians do things in their own time. Island time, as it's sometimes known. It can be infuriating. There is little-to-no sense of urgency about anything. Sardinians *always* have time to eat, drink and talk. Routine errands often take all day, as you bump into friends and end up taking *aperitivo* in the afternoon sunshine.

Cooking here reflects life; it is a slow and relaxed affair. Meat is almost always slow roasted over an open fire, often on a rustic spit, the squeaks and groans of which provide the soundtrack to many a Sardinian lunch. Cheese is made and matured slowly, using age-old methods and tools. Beans, pulses and most vegetables are cooked long and slow, extracting all their sweetness and flavour. Pasta may be *al dente*, but vegetables never. More often they are slow-cooked to a flavoursome mush. I'm an impatient person, and an extremely impatient cook. But learning from Sardinians has forced me to slow down a little. I have learnt to (mostly) enjoy it. Patience is a virtue, and one which brings its own rewards.

EAT LIKE A SARDINIAN

The Sardinian obsession with food is never self-obsessed, unhealthy or masochistic. There is no dieting culture, no fads or fashions. No paleo, protein powders or juice diets. The people of Sardinia are some of the longest-living in the world, after Japan. They are fiercely and publicly proud of this fact, attributing their longevity to their diet, their relaxed lifestyle and their strong family bonds. I personally suspect that it is also related to how much they sleep (a lot): a Sardinian's rest is sacred.

Nourishment – true nourishment – comes not from kale smoothies, but from living a balanced, happy life, and eating a balanced, varied and happy diet.

In Elizabeth David's introduction to *Italian Food* she talks about the British superstition that Italian food is 'fattening' or 'bad for you'. Not much has changed since she wrote this. Many of us avoid carbohydrates (especially bread and pasta) as we think they will make us fat.

In fact, pasta contains a high amount of protein (in the form of gluten) and starch, a complex carbohydrate. Some of the starch contained in pasta is resistant starch, which is not digested in the small intestine, but fermented in the large intestine, becoming a form of fibre. If the word 'carbohydrate,' were replaced by the word 'fibre' when referring to pasta, and the word 'gluten' replaced with 'protein' – suddenly things become very different. Pasta provides the body with protein, fibre and energy.

Every *body* is different, and no one else, nutritionist or otherwise, can tell you what really makes you feel good or healthy. However, the conversation surrounding 'health' is so saturated with conflicting, confusing advice, persuasion, emotional blackmail and bogus statistics that, rather than preach, I would only encourage you to eat what makes you happy and to enjoy foods such as pasta and bread with a clear conscience. As any Sardinian will tell you, life is for living, and food is for eating.

A NOTE ON INGREDIENTS

The core of Sardinian cooking is simplicity. Simplicity can be unforgiving.

I used to get frustrated with endless recipe books rhapsodizing about beautiful produce (mostly because I was bitter about not having access to it), but the truth is inescapable. It *is* possible to make good food with average ingredients, if you have an armoury of spices and flavourings at your disposal, but the simplicity of Sardinian food allows for no such smoke and mirrors.

Apart from sourcing the best possible raw materials, the most important thing about any kind of Italian cooking, including Sardinian, is to always use the best olive oil you can get your hands on. The other ingredients are often so cheap – pulses, pasta, grains or vegetables – that you can justify splashing out on this as your key condiment. It is the foundation of Italian cookery, and one corner that simply cannot be cut (there are others that can).

ONE

APERITIVO

Fried Sage Leaves in Beer Batter • Grilled Aubergines, Sapa,
Ricotta Salata and Mint • Roasted Pecorino, Walnuts and Honey
• *Like Sea Foam Covered in Caramel* • Music Paper Bread,
Bottarga and Olive Oil • Bottarga Pâté

APERITIVO

In Oristano, at the golden hour, when work is done and the sun is setting, people congregate in bars all over town to take an *aperitivo*; the scarlet glint of Campari rivalling the glow of the disappearing sun. It's the best part of the day, and sacred to most Sardinians.

Aperitivo is not just a drink, it's a doing and an event, and one of the best things about life in Italy. *'Prendiamo un aperitivo?'*, perhaps the equivalent of the English 'Let's have a pint?', but somehow infinitely more glamorous – I still love a pint, too. Originally derived from the Latin verb *aperire*, which means 'to open', a traditional aperitivo is a bitter drink accompanied by some salty snacks, designed to 'open' the appetite for the meal to follow.

The following dishes are all designed to be eaten at such an hour, but could also work as starters.

FRIED SAGE LEAVES IN BEER BATTER

Foglie di Salvia in Pastella alla Birra

This is one of the simplest and most satisfying of snacks. In fact, it's so simple that I wondered whether to even include it. But it has to be here, as proof that simple is often best. Fried sage leaves are also one of Franca's signature starters: her thriving sage bush being almost the only thing in the garden to survive the destructive urges of her dogs.

SERVES 6

30 or so sage leaves
400 ml (13½ fl oz/1¾ cups) mild olive, grapeseed or sunflower oil, for frying

For the batter

80 g (2¾ oz/⅔ cup) 00 flour
110 ml (3¾ fl oz/½ cup) light icy cold beer or lager
sea salt

Pick the best, even-sized and arrow-shaped sage leaves with a little length of stalk attached for holding onto. Give them a good wash in cold water and then pat dry.

In a large bowl, make a well in the flour and slowly whisk in the beer. Continue whisking until a smooth batter is formed, but don't be too vigorous, as you'll beat out all the bubbles. Add a good pinch of salt and stir gently to combine.

Heat your oil to 180°C (350°F) in a saucepan or deep-fat fryer.

Dip each leaf in the batter and swirl until evenly coated, shaking off any excess batter. Lower into the oil and fry until golden, flipping to make sure it is an even colour on both sides. Remove with a slotted spoon and place onto some kitchen paper to absorb any excess oil. Eat immediately, preferably with a glass of cold beer.

GRILLED AUBERGINES, SAPA, RICOTTA SALATA AND MINT

Melanzane Grigliate, Sapa, Ricotta Salata e Menta

Here I have played with a combination Luca and I used to make at Morito. It was a dish of fried aubergines, whipped feta and date molasses, which sold out every service. Little surprise, as it is a winning concoction of salty, fatty, silky and sweet.

If you cannot find ricotta salata, feta is a good substitute. The same goes for the sapa – you can easily use date molasses instead. The important thing is to have something sweet and syrupy against something tangy and savoury.

This dressing is so good you'll want to serve it with almost everything. It's excellent with grilled radicchio or endive (the bitterness works beautifully), or with grilled lamb and greens.

SERVES 4–6 AS AN ANTIPASTI OR SIDE DISH

80 g (2¾ oz/⅔ cup) pine nuts
3 large aubergines (eggplants), sliced into rounds, ½ cm (¼ in) thick
a handful of mint, roughly chopped
80 g (2¾ oz) ricotta salata, sliced into shards

For the dressing

1 tablespoon balsamic vinegar
1 tablespoon sapa or date molasses
1 garlic clove, minced
2 tablespoons lemon juice
zest of half a lemon, grated
5 tablespoons best-quality olive oil
pinch of chilli flakes

Preheat the oven to 170°C (340°F/Gas 4).

Tip the pine nuts onto a baking (cookie) sheet and toast for a few minutes, until golden.

In a griddle pan over a medium heat, grill the aubergines in batches until softened, making sure they take a good amount of colour on each side. Set aside.

Mix all the ingredients for the dressing and whisk well. To serve, lay the aubergine slices on a platter and sprinkle over the mint, the nuts and the ricotta. Drizzle over the dressing. This can be eaten at room temperature, warm or cold – truly, it is delicious any which way.

ROASTED PECORINO, WALNUTS AND HONEY

Pecorino Arrosto con Miele e Noci

The Sardinians love to roast, fry, melt, make, talk, taste and eat cheese. Cheese is not an ingredient: it's a way of life.

I couldn't believe it had never occurred to me before to roast cheese. Of course I've baked whole Camembert and Vacherin, and I've eaten Raclette, but I would never have thought of simply throwing a slab in a roasting tin and cooking it. How blind I've been.

Pecorino becomes irresistibly chewy when heated. Here it is spooned, oozing, onto crisp *pane carasau* sprinkled with oil and rubbed with rosemary (otherwise known as *pane guttiau*), drizzled with honey and topped with walnuts. I guarantee there is no better way to begin (or end) any meal.

There are no strict quantities for this – it's more a case of how much you want to eat.

'If in doubt, add cheese.'

SERVES ABOUT 2

2 sheets pane carasau
olive oil, for drizzling
sea salt
sprig of rosemary, leaves
  roughly chopped
4 thick slices of pecorino
  Sardo, rind removed
1 tablespoon honey
handful of walnuts

Preheat the oven to 180°C (350°F/Gas 4).

Drizzle the pane carasau with olive oil, sprinkle with sea salt and the rosemary.

Place the cheese slices in a small gratin dish and slide into the oven. On the shelf below, place the pane carasau.

When the cheese is molten and the bread golden, about 8–10 minutes for the former and 5 minutes for the latter, remove both, drizzle the cheese with honey and sprinkle over the walnuts. Serve with the bread.

LIKE SEA FOAM COVERED IN CARAMEL

Bottarga seems to epitomise Sardinia in a way that no other food stuff does: it is ancient, beautiful, other-worldly. As salty as the sea surrounding the island, and steeped in mystery and tradition.

Bottarga was introduced to Sardinia by the Phoenicians, and is still produced and eaten in large quantities today, particularly on the west coast of the island where we live. Here in the brackish lakes of Cabras, grey mullet breed and are caught and eaten, whilst their roe is made into bottarga. The sacks of roe are salted and then air-dried until they are solid and amber-coloured. Bottarga can then be grated into a sort of rust-coloured dust, or bought as a whole lobe, which you then slice or grate according to preference.

The most common way to eat it in Sardinia is either very finely grated and tossed through pasta dishes (page 116), or sliced in generous slivers and put on shards of crisp *pane carasau* with a drizzle of good olive oil (page 37). The latter is my favourite.

To those who have never tried it, the flavour is hard to describe, but it is somewhere ranging between vaguely cheesy, buttery, salty and fishy; Elizabeth Luard's description, 'like sea foam covered in caramel', is very apt. I think of it as a sort of fishy fruit gum, as it's a little chewy in texture and gets stuck in your teeth in exactly the same delicious and infuriating way. Though relatively unknown in home cooking, it is loved by chefs the world over and known as 'the sea's answer to bacon', being umami-rich and capable of adding a savoury depth to numerous dishes. Personally, I find that this comparison does bottarga a great disservice, because it is more delicious, unique and addictive than bacon – a bold claim, I realise. Saying that, it is certainly not for everyone; it is intensely, almost bitterly fishy, with a lingering mineral aftertaste and an intense savouriness found only in things like anchovies and cod's roe. For the fish lover, however, this will be a new favourite ingredient.

Though it is not cheap, even here where it is produced in large quantities, it is worth seeking out. We are lucky in that Luca's father has such a passion for the stuff that he makes his own and donates a few lobes to us every season.

Giuseppe's bottarga production is a great (and secret - until now at least) art. He salts his mullet roes at home and then rubs them down gently with a cloth dipped in a mixture of the best olive oil and Vernaccia. He then leaves them in the dark, laid out on a long table, with numerous electric fans blowing all around them, for a minimum of 20 days. He makes them in the family summer house by the sea, and leaves the windows open to allow the sea air to circulate around them as they cure, which he says improves the flavour.

The bulbous amber sacks glow in the half-light, eerie and looking like fossilised organs. When Franca takes me to see them (and turn them, they must be turned regularly) she speaks to me in hushed whisper, as though they are sentient. To Sards, they are truly sacred.

MUSIC PAPER BREAD, BOTTARGA AND OLIVE OIL

Pane Carasau, Bottarga e Olio di Oliva

This is more of an assembly than a recipe, but it is none the worse for that. I love to start a meal with thin sheets of *pane carasau*, also known as *carta di musica*, slivers of glowing, amber-coloured bottarga and a good drizzle of punchy olive oil. It's salty, crispy, sweet and bitter all at once.

SERVES 6–8

1 lobe of bottarga
4–6 sheets of pane carasau
a drizzle of best-quality extra
  virgin olive oil

Slice the bottarga with a sharp knife into 2 mm pieces and lay them on the pane carasau. Drizzle over plenty of olive oil and serve, at once, with prosecco or a dry white wine.

BOTTARGA PÂTÉ

Paté di Bottarga

I grew up eating my mum's smoked mackerel pâté (still one of my favourite things) and my granny's pastel-pink smoked trout pâté, so I was delighted to discover a Sardinian relative. Here it is served just as my mother and grandmother always served fish pâté, on little earthenware dishes sprinkled with cayenne. For all the fancy canapés and fiddly 'nibbles' in the world, you really can't beat a fat blob of salty fish pâté on a crisp piece of bread – to my mind, at least.

There is no added salt in this recipe as the bottarga, tuna and anchovies are all salty. Taste and see if you'd like to add some, though.

SERVES 6 AS A (VERY RICH) STARTER

80 g (2¾ oz) bottarga
   (whole or grated), plus extra
   to serve (optional)
80 g (2¾ oz) tinned tuna,
   drained
8 anchovy fillets
200 g (7 oz) unsalted butter
pinch of cayenne
   or chilli powder
squeeze of lemon juice
   (optional)
chive or mint flowers, to serve
   (optional)

Blend the bottarga, tuna and anchovies in a mixer until completely smooth. Add the butter and blend the whole lot again until you have a lovely creamy smooth pâté.

Place in the fridge to firm up a little. Let it soften a little before serving, you don't want it rock hard. Serve in little dishes topped with extra grated bottarga or cayenne pepper, a squeeze of lemon juice and some chive or mint flowers.

TWO

MERENDA

Yoghurt Cake Three Ways • *Black as Night and Thick as Soup* •
Blood Orange, Ricotta, Polenta and Olive Oil Cake • *Green Gold*
• Ripe Pears and Pecorino • Ricotta, Figs, Thyme and Honey •
Pane con Burro e Acciughe

MERENDA

Patience Gray wrote of the snack being 'snatched' whilst the *merenda* is 'shared'. It's a lovely notion, and one which still exists in Sardinian culture. Snacking in England often holds all sorts of negative, guilty associations, but the merenda in Italy, like almost every other opportunity to eat, is a true event, and celebrated for this. The morning merenda is taken at 11 a.m. or thereabouts, and the afternoon one at 4 p.m. So perhaps it is the Italian equivalent of (the now nearly extinct) elevenses and high tea.

Merenda in Sardinia can take the form of small cakes, leftover dolci, fruit, or simply a piece of bread with salami or cheese.

The following recipes are some of my favourite things to snack on.

YOGHURT CAKE THREE WAYS

Ciambellone in Tre Modi

Also known simply as 'yoghurt cake', almost every nonna in Italy will make a version of this recipe, which must be the easiest and most versatile cake in history.

There is something nostalgic and comforting about a very simple, soft and springy sponge cake, with its golden crust and butter-yellow crumb. The English have Victoria sponge; the Italians have *ciambellone*.

Usually baked in a bundt or ring tin, the method involves using a small yoghurt pot of 125 ml or 150 ml (4¼ fl oz or 5 fl oz) to measure every ingredient into the mixing bowl, starting with the yoghurt itself.

It is ideal for breakfast, its uncomplicated sweetness balancing a coffee perfectly.

This is Franca's recipe. She does not bake. Ever. Except this, which she knows is fool-proof. A cake for baking-haters then, too. The method is wonderfully slap-dash, and totally forgiving. If only baking could always be thus.

MAKES 26 CM (10 IN) RING TIN CAKE

NOTE

Here in Sardinia, the baking powder comes in ready-to-use 16 g (½ oz) sachets. For some reason it is always pre-flavoured with vanilla. If you replace it with a drop of vanilla extract you will achieve a similar result.

continued overleaf →

ORIGINAL YOGHURT CAKE

melted butter, for greasing
3 'pots' plain (all-purpose) flour,
    plus a little extra for dusting
1 x 125 ml or 150 ml (4¼ fl oz or 5 fl oz)
    pots natural (plain) yoghurt
2 'pots' caster (superfine) sugar
1 'pot' sunflower oil
3 eggs
zest of 1 lemon
zest of 1 orange
3 teaspoons baking powder
few drops of vanilla extract (see note on previous page)

Preheat the oven to 180°C (350°F/Gas 4).

Using a pastry brush, grease the cake tin with the melted butter, then shake a little flour around to coat the inside.

Decant all of the yoghurt into a blender or stand mixer. Use the same pot to measure the sugar and the oil, then add to the yoghurt one by one – you don't need to rinse it between measuring. Add the eggs, lemon zest and orange zest, the baking powder and the vanilla and blitz until smooth.

Pour into the prepared tin and bake for 40–50 minutes, until risen and firm to the touch. Allow to cool in the tin for a few minutes, then turn out and let cool completely on a wire rack. This will keep in an airtight container for up to 6 days.

YOGHURT CAKE WITH APPLE

An excellent way of using up some forgotten fruit-bowl apples, though so good it's worth buying them especially, too.

Follow the recipe for the original yoghurt cake, but add 150 g (5¼ oz) apple, peeled and cut into pebble-sized pieces, to the mix.

This enhances the moistness of the cake and makes it somehow more appropriate for breakfast by adding some nutritional value (an English preoccupation, rather than a Sardinian one).

POMEGRANATE YOGHURT CAKE

Pomegranates grow well in Sardinia, and I am always looking for new ways to use them. This is an excellent way of dressing up the simplest cake in history and making it look like you've gone to lots of trouble when you haven't. Domed and jewel-crested, it's the perfect thing to impress your guests, or to take to others. Whenever called upon to provide a cake for any *feste* here (and there are many) this is what I bring. There is something wonderful about the way the pomegranate juice dyes the icing such a vivid colour without the necessity of any artificial colouring. To make the icing, you'll need 2 pomegranates; squeeze half of one into a bowl and whisk with 150 g (5¼ oz) icing (confectioners') sugar to make an icing. Deseed the remaining one and a half pomegranates, glaze the cake with the icing and then scatter over the seeds with abandon.

BLACK AS NIGHT AND THICK AS SOUP

The sounds of Sardinia waking up; the 'shake shake' of a sugar packet, the background whirr of the grinder and a sighing *'phoo'* of steam. Stubby white cups of espresso are the life-blood of Italy.

Coffee arrived in Europe via Venice, brought by the Arabs, and the first coffee shop opened there in 1640.

According to many Italians, real espresso doesn't exist outside Italy, and despite my vain attempts to initiate Luca into London coffee culture, he would always slam down his cup in disgust. Whether you agree with Luca or not, there is something quintessentially Italian about an espresso, and the café culture in general is a source of great amusement and enjoyment to a foreigner like me. The Italian snobbery about coffee is so prevalent that I had to abandon my love of filter coffee and 'flat whites' as soon as I moved here, and force myself to become sophisticated enough to only drink espresso.

BLOOD ORANGE, RICOTTA, POLENTA AND OLIVE OIL CAKE

Torta di Arancia Sanguigna, Ricotta, Polenta e Olio di Oliva

A perfect cake, this is simultaneously fluffy, rich and light. The polenta gives it a lovely crunchiness at the edges. It will stay soft and sticky for days, though it is unlikely it will last that long – it is especially delicious for breakfast with an espresso. Blood oranges look the most striking with their scarlet flesh, but normal oranges will work just as well. A final note: this batter will look very runny when it is made, but do not be alarmed. It is all exactly as you planned...

SERVES 8–10

For the base

1–2 blood oranges
100 g (3½ oz/½ cup) demerara sugar

For the batter

200 ml (6¾ fl oz/¾ cup) olive oil, plus extra for greasing
200 g (7 oz/1 cup) caster (superfine) sugar
pinch of sea salt
250 g (8¾ oz) ricotta
zest and juice of 4 small blood oranges
juice and zest of 1 large lemon
4 eggs
100 g (3½ oz/⅔ cup) polenta
150 g (5¼ oz/1¼ cups) plain (all-purpose) flour
2 teaspoons baking powder

Preheat the oven to 180°C (350°F/Gas 4). Grease and line a 20 cm (8 in) cake tin.

First, prepare the base of the cake. Wash the oranges and slice them into 2 mm discs with a very sharp knife (you can use a mandoline or a slicer if you have them). I leave the rind on, as when cooked like this it becomes edible, but if you prefer you can remove it.

In a small saucepan over a medium heat, melt the demerara sugar with 2 tablespoons water until it has dissolved. Simmer for a few minutes until the syrup begins to caramelise (you should smell and see the colour change to a light amber). Pour your syrup over the bottom of the cake tin. Arrange the slices of blood orange, as many as will fit in one layer in a pleasing pattern, on top of the syrup.

To make the batter, whisk the oil, sugar, salt, ricotta, citrus juice and zest together in a large mixing bowl. Add in the eggs one at a time and beat until smooth. Add in the dry ingredients and beat until smooth. Pour the batter into the prepared tin and bake for 40–50 minutes, until golden and just set.

Allow the cake to cool for 5 minutes, then run a knife around the edge of the tin and invert onto a wire rack or serving plate. Allow to cool completely before slicing.

GREEN GOLD

Mediterranean cuisine is based on three essential plants: wheat, vines and olives. These basic crops give the very best things in life, three things which remain the pillars of Sardinian cuisine: bread, wine and olive oil. Olives have been picked and eaten since 8,000 BC – they make Christianity look young – and olive oil was produced as early as 4,000 BC.

Olive oil is not just a seasoning or a means of frying, but a beautiful product in its own right. If I have decent olive oil in the house, I know I can make something good to eat, whether it's just bread and olive oil, pasta with olive oil, or a simple salad.

The Romans had a reverence for olive oil like my own. Besides eating it, they used it as a remedy, as a lubricant and as a moisturiser. A typical Roman breakfast consisted of a sort of savoury porridge drizzled with olive oil. And to this day, olive oil has a religious significance; in the Roman Catholic church, babies' foreheads are anointed with olive oil during baptism.

The process of producing olive oil hasn't changed much in the last few thousand years. Olives are harvested (often still by hand, by vigorously shaking the trees), washed and then pressed, either in a special machine or between granite stones. This first pressing produces what we know as 'extra virgin' olive oil. The resulting liquid (a mixture of oil and watery juice) is then separated and the olive oil is bottled.

Recently olive oil has slightly fallen out of favour, as more fashionable fats such as coconut oil take centre-stage. However, the nutritional benefits of this substance cannot be challenged. Olive oil is composed of essential fatty acids and antioxidants, and has been proven to both lower blood pressure, prevent heart disease, and even decrease the risk of Alzheimer's.

Cooking in Sardinia means using two different olive oils; one good, the best extra virgin you can afford, and one 'bad' – still extra virgin but cheap-ish. The bad one is used for cooking, and the good one for drizzling and dressing. The flavour of the good one is an essential part of the finished dish.

Sardinian olive oil does not have much of a reputation abroad, though I'm unsure why, as it rivals the best of Ligurian oils in flavour. It tastes very like the artichokes that grow so well here; grassy, slightly tannic and bittersweet.

RIPE PEARS AND PECORINO

Pere e Pecorino

More a suggestion than a recipe, the contrast of sweet, juicy pears and salty, sharp pecorino is hard to beat. Like all of the simplest assemblies, this dish relies on the perfection of both of its elements. You need an exceptional pear, heavy with juice and still cool from a morning sitting, waiting to be chosen, at the autumn market. Then you need good, buttery, crumbly, aged pecorino Sardo. Eat a bite of one, then the other, with the juice dripping down your chin.

'Do not let the peasant know how good the cheese is with the pears.'

— ITALIAN PROVERB

RICOTTA, FIGS, THYME AND HONEY

Ricotta, Fichi, Timo e Miele

If you are going to snack, then make sure you snack well. Jammy-sweet black figs, mellowed by creamy ricotta and piled atop some charred toast with a drizzle of oil and honey: this is a snack of the gods. Best eaten alone.

SERVES 1

2 slices of good-quality sourdough bread
100 g (3½ oz) ricotta
4 ripe black figs
olive oil, for drizzling
1 tablespoon honey
sea salt
sprig of thyme

Toast your bread and spread with the ricotta. Tear the figs and arrange them on top. Drizzle over the oil and the honey and sprinkle over the salt. Rub the thyme between your fingers to scatter the leaves over the top. Eat.

PANE CON BURRO E ACCIUGHE

Bread, butter and anchovies

Many (though I hope not all) will recognise this as one of life's greatest mouthfuls. For those who are already devotees, I can only give you my thoughts on this simple but sensational combination. For those of you who have never tried it, I hope after reading this you will be inspired to do so.

This is what I eat when there is nothing else in the house, or when I'm feeling too lazy to go shopping. And every time I eat it, I wonder why I bother eating anything else anyway. In a world where nothing is seemingly perfect, this just is. Perfection, however, means attention to detail; the 'recipe', or rather advice on ingredients, is this:

The bread must have a chewy, giving crumb, and a crisp, dark crust. It must be white-ish and uncomplicated, none of your fancy granary or heritage rye here. The butter must be cold, pure chalky white, unsalted, sliced very thick, like cheese. It must be placed – not spread – on the bread. The anchovies must be very fat and juicy, draped liberally over the cool, marble-white butter slabs, like shining pilgrims prostrate at an altar. That's it.

THREE

VERDURE

VERDURE

The Sardinians are very puritanical about their vegetables, and claim the quality is so high they must rarely be tampered with. Good olive oil and salt are often the only seasonings (sometimes not even these) whether the vegetables are cooked or raw, and are said to enhance rather than confuse the flavour.

The vegetables here are so good they are worthy of celebration, and of the reverence the Sards bestow on them. There is a mountain potato (the *Patate de Gavoi*), for instance, from a region in central Sardinia, that is so famously good it has its own festival. When these arrive at the market, we eat a whole dish of them simply boiled, peeled and dressed with peppery olive oil and sea salt. They are yellow and sticky, and taste of sugar and soil.

The Sardinian methods of cooking vegetables came as a surprise to me. Whilst pasta is always *al dente*, it is a myth peddled by the English that Italians cook their vegetables with bite. There is no such middle-ground. Here vegetables tend to be treated in two distinct ways; either eaten crisp and raw, or cooked long and slow until completely tender.

CRUDO

Never underestimate the deliciousness of raw vegetables. The crudité, that sad remnant of 1970s drinks parties in Britain, is still very much alive and well in Sardinia. Known instead as *pinzimonio*, washed, peeled and sliced raw vegetables form an important part of almost every meal. Served on oval white dishes, cool and shining from their recent cold bath, they are celebrated for the beautiful things they are.

Tomatoes, when in season, are served whole, with oil and salt provided for you to slice and dress as you please. Lettuce too, is simply washed, shredded and plonked on the table. Fennel is often served unadorned, after meat, in thick, cold, crisp slices, to clean the palate. Little ceremony, much flavour.

COTTO

There are countless leafy bitter greens grown here that flood the markets throughout the winter; endive, chicory and dandelions of all descriptions. They are boiled well, in plenty of salted water, then cooled and drained, served cold and dressed with good olive oil. Wild chard, cultivated chard and spinach, too, is treated in this manner. It may sound odd, but cold, cooked and drained spinach and chard dressed with a punchy olive oil and salt is one of the most surprisingly delicious things you will ever eat. The iron-rich, green flavour of these plants is best appreciated in this way.

Aubergines (eggplants), (bell) peppers, and courgettes (zucchini) are stuffed and baked, deep-fried, or cooked long and slow in plenty of oil. Artichokes (if not eaten raw) are stuffed, baked, braised or sautéed.

The sort of slow-cooked vegetable dishes that involve a lot of olive oil, such as Slow-cooked courgettes (page 76), serve various purposes. Frequently made in large batches, they can be made in advance, and often improve with age. They appear as *antipasti*, as a light lunch with some bread and cheese, or as a side dish for meat. Then, at last, in a final flourish, they are transformed into delicious sauces for pasta.

HOW TO EAT
AN ARTICHOKE

*'The artichoke above all is the expression of civilised living, of
the long view, of increasing delight by anticipation and crescendo.'*
— JANE GRIGSON

You may, like I once foolishly did, think artichokes are a lot of hassle for
little reward. In my former life as a chef, I had to prep hundreds of these
spiky vegetables, and I never really thought the end result justified the
effort. That was until I moved here, and I discovered how to eat (and how
to cook) artichokes.

ARTICHOKES
IN SARDINIA

The two main varieties grown
here are the *tema* and the *spinoso*.
The tema can be found all over
Italy; they have short spines (the
spikes at the tip of each petal)
and a more purple hue in comparison
to the greener spinoso. Their season
lasts from October to April. The
Spinoso variety have a shorter,
sweeter season. They appear in late
October and disappear again sometimes
in just a month. Occasionally they
reappear again after Christmas, in
the early spring. Green all over,
with an elongated bud and lethal long
yellow spines at the tip of each
petal, this artichoke is famed for
its unique tenderness and perfect
balance of bitter and sweet. It has

DOP status, and grows particularly
well here due to the special
composition of Sardinian soil.

In terms of nutrition too, the
artichoke is worth looking closely
at. Artichokes have one of the
highest antioxidant levels of
any vegetable (some studies claim
the highest) and are also packed
with minerals and fibre. They
are particularly high in inulin,
a dietary fibre and prebiotic.

Perhaps, then, if we all ate
an artichoke a day, rather than
an apple (as the proverb has it)
we too would live as long as
the Sardinians.

THE EATING

The very best way to eat an artichoke, it turns out, is not to cook it at all. When the season arrives, I eat one or two a day, until they disappear again. The moment the spiny specimens arrive at the market, I simply put them in a vase of water in the centre of the table, like a bunch of flowers (which is, after all, what they are, or – more precisely – thistles).

We each help ourselves to one, and peel it slowly with a knife. Next to us is a bowl with good olive oil and some sea salt in it. The stem of the 'choke is peeled of the fibrous outer bits, until the paler, smooth, tender inner-stem remains. This is then cut into pieces, dunked in the oil and eaten. Next the flower head is peeled, petal by petal, each being dunked again into the oil, and the bottom (where the yellow flesh is) gnawed. Finally, we reach the heart, protected by a pale violet fur – the soft reminder of the artichoke's thistle lineage. Scrape or cut away this fluff, and beneath lies a perfect, nutty, tender heart. This we cut into chunks and eat with more oil and salt.

There is a ritualistic element to this that I love. Everyone silent and concentrating, busily peeling their artichokes. It's like eating a whole crab: there is activity, labour, and then frequent, tiny and sweet nuggets of reward. This is my favourite sort of food, and my favourite way to eat.

THE COOKING

When it comes to cooking them, there is no escaping the fact that preparing them is laborious. A little patience can be a good thing, and the result is always worth it.

The preparation of artichokes - at least how far you go in preparing them - depends on what they are destined for. For those recipes where they are eaten by being pulled apart petal by petal, very little preparation is necessary, as some of the labour manifests in the eating. If you want to eat them in their entirety, or prepare them fully, without having to pick at them with fingers such as in the recipe on page 66, then this is how to do it.

HOW TO PREPARE AN ARTICHOKE

Prepare a large, deep bowl full of cold water and squeeze into it the juice of 2 lemons (you can leave the halves in the bowl).

Take the artichoke and begin to rip away the outer leaves from the bud. Rip away and discard about two full layers of outer petals, until you can see a greater deal of the yellow inner petals, closed tightly in a bud.

Using a swivel peeler, peel away the coarser outside of the base and stem, until the paler, smoother flesh is exposed.

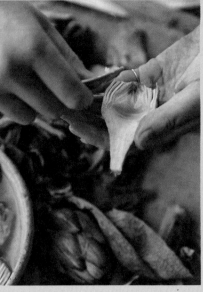

Using a sharp knife, cut
the whole tip of the bud off,
aiming about halfway down the
bud. Discard these tips.

Now, cut the choke in
half lengthways, and using
a teaspoon, scoop out the
fluffy choke.

Place the halves in the
acidulated water until ready
to cook.

PRESERVED ARTICHOKES

Carciofini Sott'olio

These are the ubiquitous antipasti in Sardinia; a way of celebrating the extraordinary quality of the local artichokes. We make them with the artichokes in the late spring, which are particularly small and tender.

When you get shop- or deli-bought artichokes under oil they are often soggy, flabby, flavourless and oil-sodden, but this recipe ensures that they remain firm and entire, with a deliciously acidic bite to them. The trick is the sunflower oil. After extensive experimentation (Franca and Gianni make these and compare notes every year) they discovered that preserving them under olive oil makes them soft, whereas preserving them under sunflower oil keeps them firm. If you are fastidious about the taste of sunflower oil, you can always drain the chokes before serving, and drizzle with a good olive oil instead.

They are fiddly to make, and will take up most of a day, but are well worth it, as the jars can be given as gifts or kept to serve throughout the year with thin slices of prosciutto and crusty bread.

Franca loves the purity of artichokes so much she doesn't add any herbs, but I know those who add oregano or bay or garlic cloves. The choice is yours.

MAKES 2 LARGE JARS

1 kg (2 lb 3¼ oz) small artichokes
500 ml (17 fl oz/2 cups) white wine
200 ml (7 fl oz/¾ cup) white wine vinegar
700 ml (24 fl oz/3 cups) sunflower oil
bay leaves, garlic, rosemary or another herb of your choice

Prepare the artichokes as described on page 64.

Put the wine, vinegar and 300 ml (10 fl oz/1¼ cups) water in a large pan and bring to the boil. Drop the prepared artichokes into the liquid and cook for 2 minutes. Fish them out with a slotted spoon and lay them out to dry on a tea towel. Cover with another cloth and leave them to dry for half an hour or so.

Sterilise your jars by boiling them in water or putting them through the dishwasher on the highest setting.

Heat the oil to 80°C (175°F); at this point add your herbs, if using, into the jars. Fill the jars half full with the oil, then place inside as many artichokes as you can fit. Top with oil and screw the cap on tightly. All the artichokes must be completely submerged. These will then keep like this for years.

STUFFED ARTICHOKES

Carciofi Ripieni

Another reason to love artichokes. In this recipe they are cooked as whole flowers, which makes a great (and vegetarian!) centrepiece. The stuffing is tucked between the petals and then they are baked in the oven, so that all of their delicious juices run down into the bread and garlic stuffing to create a flavourful, juicy, soggy bottom and a crispy, cheesy top – the best of both worlds.

The flowers are then eaten with fingers, sucking petal by petal, to which clings a little of the stuffing until you reach the heart, and then – even better – the bits stuck to the bottom of the dish. This amalgamation of garlicky oil, artichoke juice and breadcrumbs is then mopped up with even more bread. The flavour and texture is wonderfully reminiscent of the kind of garlic bread I ate as a child, with finely chopped parsley and part soggy, part crispy, fat-soaked white bread.

Serve as a starter alone, or with a green salad and fresh bread for a simple main course.

SERVES 4 AS A STARTER OR 2 AS A MAIN

4 medium artichokes
2 small garlic cloves, minced
60 g (2 oz) pecorino or
  Parmesan, grated
a handful of chopped parsley
pinch of lemon zest
160 g (5½ oz/1 cup) fine
  breadcrumbs
sea salt
6 tablespoons extra virgin
  olive oil

Choose a gratin dish where your artichokes will fit snugly and preheat the oven to 180°C (350°F/Gas 4). Chop off any of the stalk so that just the heads remain and peel away the tough outer leaves. If you like, you can also snip off the spiky tips of each petal with scissors, though often I don't bother. Next – the therapeutic bit – pick up the artichokes and bash them on the worktop, spiky petal-side down. Do this a few times until the flowers open up (this will make more space for your stuffing to sit).

Arrange the buds in the gratin dish, petals pointing upwards.

In a mixing bowl, combine the garlic, cheese, chopped parsley, lemon zest and breadcrumbs. Add a good pinch of salt and mix again. Taste for seasoning.

Sprinkle the stuffing all over the artichokes, making sure to get it into all the gaps between petals and in the centre. If you have any surplus, sprinkle it over the bottom of the dish. Now drizzle over the oil and pour 350 ml (12 fl oz/1½ cups) water into the bottom of the dish. Bake for 35–45 minutes, making sure to top up the liquid if it boils dry. The artichokes are done when they are tender to the touch and when the petals pull off with very little resistance.

Serve in the gratin dish, with extra bread for mopping and a green salad, if you like.

ARTICHOKES BRAISED WITH SAGE, LEMON, FENNEL AND OLIVES WITH SAFFRON AIOLI

Carciofi, Finocchi, Olive, Pomodori in Umido con Aioli di Zafferano

Based on a lovely vegetarian dish we made at Spring, where both Luca and I worked for a time, before leaving London. This dish is a sort of Mediterranean medley, with echoes of North Africa, Italy, and Southern France. It feels a fitting reflection of Sardinia's many culinary influences and makes the perfect vegetarian main course.

Whilst mayonnaise is common in Sardinian cooking, aioli seems to have made its way around other parts of the Mediterranean, but not yet here. As the name derives from the Catalan for 'garlic and oil', and there is plenty of Catalan heritage here (most specifically the former Catalan colony of Alghero), it feels right to include it. The tyranny of staying 'true' to a recipe's origins should never come between you and a good thing.

SERVES 4–6

5 tablespoons olive oil
2 garlic cloves, sliced
3 large fennel bulbs, topped, tailed and cut into eighths lengthways
2 dried red chillies
1 teaspoon fennel seeds
10 sage leaves
6–8 whole artichokes, prepped as described on page 64 and halved
500 g (1 lb 1¾ oz) tomatoes, chopped (or tinned)
120 ml (4 fl oz/½ cup) white wine
3 strips of lemon zest
100 g (3½ oz) purple or small black olives
5 fresh bay leaves
¼ lemon, segmented and chopped
sea salt
pinch of caster (superfine) sugar
1 bunch of parsley, chopped

In a wide lidded frying pan, heat the oil. Cook the garlic until fragrant, then add the fennel slices, the chilli and the fennel seeds. Cook over a medium heat until the fennel just begins to catch and take colour, around 5 minutes, then add the sage leaves. Cook for another minute or two, stirring, then add the prepped artichokes. Stir everything until it is coated with the oil and cook for a few minutes, until the artichokes too begin to turn light golden.

Add the tomatoes, wine and strips of lemon zest. Cover and cook over a low heat for 40 minutes, until the fennel and artichokes are tender and the tomatoes and wine have formed a thick sauce. Add the olives, the bay and lemon segments, followed by the salt and sugar to taste. Stir and simmer for another 5 minutes. Add the chopped parsley.

For the saffron aioli

2 egg yolks
¼ teaspoon saffron strands
  soaked in 2 tablespoons
  hot water
1 scant teaspoon sea salt
1 teaspoon mustard (optional)
2 garlic cloves, minced
200 ml (7 fl oz/¾ cup) best-
  quality extra virgin olive oil
100 ml (3½ fl oz/scant
  ½ cup) neutral oil,
  such as sunflower
2 tablespoons lemon juice

To make the aioli, place the yolks and saffron with its soaking water in a small bowl or the jug of a blender. Add the salt, mustard (if using) and garlic and start whisking. Drizzle the oil in drop by drop until it is emulsified, blitzing or whisking vigorously all the while. Add the lemon. Mix and taste for seasoning. Add more lemon or salt according to your preference. If you like, dilute with a little cold water to make it runnier.

Spoon the braised artichokes onto plates and serve with a spoonful of aioli on top.

FENNEL GRATIN

Finocchi Gratinati

There are few things that aren't better when baked in a creamy sauce and cooked under the grill until crisp on top. Gratins are instant crowd-pleasers, and so simple to put together. The two main ways to make a gratin are with a traditional béchamel, or with a simple cream reduction, the latter of which is used in this recipe. I love béchamel, but the delicacy of fennel seems to work better this way.

A staple vegetable in Sardinia, fennel provides a clean and fresh flavour throughout the year. This is a wonderful way of using them in winter, and is delicious served with steak, fish or roast pork, or even just on its own.

This dish is based on something I always order at one of my favourite restaurants in Devon, The Sea Horse. It is served in dainty little silver dishes and is beautifully pale and elegant. It has a quiet, creamy purity that I love.

SERVES 4 AS A MAIN OR 6 AS A SIDE

butter, for greasing
3 fennel bulbs, sliced to ½ cm
   (¼ in) thickness
350 ml (5 fl oz/1½ cups)
   double (heavy) cream
1 garlic clove, bashed
sea salt
pinch of grated nutmeg
50 g (1¾ oz) Parmesan, grated
30 g (1 oz/scant ¼ cup)
   breadcrumbs

Preheat the oven to 190°C (375°F/Gas 5). Generously butter a medium-sized gratin dish.

Bring a pan of salted water to the boil. Drop in the fennel slices and cook for two minutes, until just translucent, but not floppy. Drain well, pat dry with paper and lay them in a buttered gratin dish.

Heat the cream with the garlic clove in a small saucepan and bring almost to the boil – at which point, take off the heat and set aside to infuse for 10 minutes. After this time, fish out the garlic and season the cream with salt and nutmeg, tasting as you go. Add a third of the cheese and stir until incorporated. Pour the cream over the fennel.

Sprinkle the breadcrumbs and the rest of the Parmesan over the top and bake in the oven for around 25 minutes, until golden and bubbling.

SLOW-COOKED FLAT BEANS WITH TOMATO, PANCETTA AND CHILLI

Fagiolini Piatti in Umido con Pomodori, Pancetta e Peperoncino

There are versions of this dish made all over Italy (and beyond – I've made a Persian one before when working at Morito). It's a simple concept, and endlessly satisfying to eat; sloppy, noodle-soft beans in a rich, slurping tomato sauce.

The Sardinian version of course contains added pig in the form of pancetta or guanciale, but you can easily make this vegetarian by omitting it.

It keeps well in the fridge and is even better the day after. I like to eat it as a good simple lunch with some bread and cheese.

SERVES 6

1 small white onion, sliced
4 tablespoons olive oil
1 dried red chilli
1 bay leaf
50 g (1¾ oz) diced pancetta
   or guanciale (optional)
500 g (1 lb 1½ oz) flat beans,
   topped, tailed and cut into
   10 cm (4 in) lengths
500 g (1 lb 1½ oz) tinned
   or fresh chopped tomatoes
sea salt
basil leaves, to serve

In a frying pan (skillet) over a medium heat, cook the onions in the olive oil with the chilli and bay leaf. Add the pancetta (if using). Continue to cook until just turning golden.

Add the beans to the pot and stir to coat them in the oil. Next, add the tomatoes and turn the heat to a low simmer. Cook for 30–40 minutes, until the beans are soft and the tomatoes have formed a rich sauce. Season and serve, scattered with basil leaves.

VERDURE

SLOW-COOKED COURGETTES WITH MINT, CHILLI AND ALMONDS

Zucchine con Menta e Mandorle

The courgette (zucchini), like the aubergine (eggplant), is something the Italians understand well. They know that liberal oil is the key to unlocking the sweet nuttiness of this water-heavy vegetable. In this recipe, the courgettes are cooked long and slow, in plenty of olive oil, with a sprinkling of dried chilli and lots of finely sliced garlic. The resulting luxurious combination is delicious on its own, served with a scattering of mint and some toasted almonds as a stand-alone dish, or as a silky bed on which to pile pork chops or roast chicken. After eating them like this, you'll never think ill of a courgette again. I love mint here, but any soft herb is good (dill, tarragon, basil or parsley).

I can taste almonds in courgettes. If you try this combination, maybe you will not think me completely mad.

SERVES 4–6

5 tablespoons olive oil
3 garlic cloves, finely sliced
700 g courgettes (zucchini), halved and thinly sliced widthways
1 dried chilli, crumbled, or a pinch of chilli flakes
sea salt
handful of mint leaves, chopped
pinch of lemon zest
2 tablespoons almonds, toasted and chopped roughly

In a heavy lidded frying pan (skillet) over a medium heat, warm the oil and then add the garlic and the courgettes. Add the chilli and cook over a medium-low heat, stirring occasionally, so that the courgettes begin to take some colour and caramelize.

After 5–10 minutes, when a fair few of the courgettes have caramelized, place the lid of the pan on and turn the heat down. Cook for another 10 minutes, stirring occasionally; if they begin to catch, add a splash of water.

Once softened, taste and season. Add the chopped mint, lemon zest and almonds just before serving. This is best eaten at room temperature, with crusty bread and cheese.

SUFFOCATED CAULIFLOWER

Cavolfiore Soffocato

There is so much more to cauliflower than the wan, sodden florets I remember from schooldays. When cooked in this way (and how can anyone resist a recipe with such a name?) the Cinderella of the cabbage world is finally allowed to go to the ball, and show herself nutty and sweet enough to rival them all.

Really one of the simplest recipes I have ever known. If you wish to liven up the colour a little you can add chopped parsley, but I like the beige-ness of it. It's a great side dish for chicken and pork, or you can just serve with bread, cheese and a few more olives.

SERVES 4–6

1 medium cauliflower,
   broken into florets
3 tablespoons extra virgin
   olive oil
130 g (4½ oz) green olives
sea salt, to taste

In a wide, lidded frying pan, cook the cauliflower in the oil over medium heat, until just beginning to colour. Add 4 tablespoons water and simmer until the cauliflower is completely tender. Now add the olives and cook for a few minutes more. Taste the sauce for seasoning and add a pinch of salt, if necessary.

NOTE

If you have good olives in brine, you can use it as some of the liquid for braising your cauliflower. If you so, be careful about how much salt you add later.

BAKED CARDOONS WITH PARMESAN AND BUTTER

Cardi Gratinati al Burro

A cardoon is a funny-looking thing, like an illegitimate child of a dragon and a celery bulb. These stalky, spiky vegetables are close relations of both the thistle and the artichoke. It is the ridged stems that are eaten, which have a nutty, grassy, slightly tannic flavour. I love them. They are not too hard to find if you look for them, and the Sardinians cook them often. They appear just at the bleakest time of year when other vegetables are sparse. This dish is a testament to the truth that there are few things in life that are not made even more delicious by the addition of butter and Parmesan.

This is also very good with some chopped walnuts sprinkled over before baking.

SERVES 4 AS A SIDE DISH OR STARTER

2 cardoon heads
50 g (1¾ oz) butter
50 g (1¾ oz) Parmesan, grated
20 g (¾ oz) walnuts, roughly
  chopped (optional)
sea salt

First, preheat the oven to 190°C (375°F/Gas 5).

The cooking of the cardoons is very straightforward, but the preparation is a little laborious. Discard the toughest, outermost stalks. Chop off the root and reserve (this can be peeled of its outer stumps to its tender heart and eaten raw, dunked in good oil and salt). Using a peeler, peel away the stringy ridges and edges of the outer, larger stalks. With a clean, damp scourer or a brush, rub away the cloudy layer on the stalks inside and out, under a running tap.

Go over each stalk well, making sure all the stringiest bits and spiky bits have been peeled away. It should now be green, smooth, and look much like a clean stick of celery. Cut into 8 cm (3 in) lengths.

Meanwhile, bring a large pan of salted water to the boil. Drop in the cardoon stalks and cook until just tender, around 8–10 minutes. Remove and drain well. When completely dry, place the cardoons in a gratin dish. Dot the butter on top and sprinkle over the Parmesan. Bake for 10 minutes, until golden brown and bubbling.

VINO SARDO

Sardinian wines are not well known or often found outside Sardinia, which is a shame, because they are very good.

Vermentino was introduced to the island in the 18th century, and those made in Gallura now have a DOCG status. Sardinian Vermentino wines are crisp and refreshing with a faintly bitter-almond aftertaste. They are also delicious paired with the many seafood dishes of the island.

VERNACCIA AND VERNACCIA DI ORISTANO DOC

Vernaccia is an indigenous Sardinian grape, the name deriving from the Latin, *vernaculus*, which means indigenous.

Vernaccia di Oristano DOC is a variety of fortified wine produced only in the mid-west region of Sardinia, around our town of Oristano, in the valley of the Tirso river. Though the wine was not granted DOC status until 1971, it is of ancient origin, and is mentioned in historical texts dating back to the 14th century. Eleanora D'Arborea, Oristano's first lady, is responsible for encouraging and controlling the production of Vernaccia in this region.

Vernaccia is made in a similar way to sherry; the grapes are harvested late when they are almost overripe and bursting with sugar. The wine is then put into chestnut barrels which are not quite filled, allowing oxygen in the air to interact naturally with the wine. A layer of yeast known as 'flor' forms on top of the wine and imparts it with its unique flavour. The Vernaccia is then aged for a minimum of four years.

Vernaccia is mostly drunk either as an aperitif or all day long during one of the many festivals that happen throughout the year. It is rich, mellow and amber-coloured, tasting of bitter-almonds; drink it in small sherry-style glasses (small because it is deceptively strong).

It is also used widely in cooking, and like its Spanish cousin, sherry, is particularly good with seafood. Instead of white wine, a glug of Vernaccia in a seafood stew or pasta sauce, or over a roasting fish is always delicious - the toasty almond notes enhance the sweetness of the flesh. I use it in almost everything; it adds a complexity, acidity and richness that white wine frequently lacks.

If you cannot find Vernaccia, substitute with a good medium (neither sweet nor too dry) sherry.

CANNONAU

Cannonau is Sardinia's most famous red wine, though it is rarely found outside the island. The grape, which is known as Grenache in France or Garnacha is Spain, was thought to have been introduced by the Aragonese in the 14th Century. Recent archaeological studies, however, have discovered remains of vines dating back to 3,200 years ago, which suggest that the grape is in fact indigenous to Sardinia, and that Cannonau is the oldest wine in the Mediterranean basin. The Sards are, of course, delighted by this discovery.

Cannonau wines are rich, full-bodied reds that pair perfectly with the equally rich game, ragùs and cheeses of Sardinia. The Cannonau grape produces wines that are typically berry flavoured, spicy, soft on the palate and have a relatively high alcoholic content. To be classified as a Cannonau wine it must be aged for at least one year, and be above 13 per cent alcohol.

The longevity of the Sardinian people, which I have alluded to frequently, is often attributed to their enthusiastic consumption of this particular wine. Most Sardinians drink one or two glasses of Cannonau a day with their meals, occasionally shop-bought, but more frequently made at home or gifted from a friend.

In this way, their health and longevity seems to mirror what is commonly known as the 'French Paradox': a phenomenon (now much explored) that highlights the lack of coronary heart disease in French people despite a diet rich in saturated fats (cheese etc.). The explanation most often put forward for this is a high consumption of red wine. Cannonau wines are especially high in phenols and antioxidants, which are considered to be beneficial for coronary health.

PASTA AND POTATOES IN BROTH

Minestra con le Patate

This is one of Nonna Giulia's staples; her motto, *'poveri ma belli'* (translating as 'poor but beautiful') manifested in edible form. It is one of the simplest dishes imaginable. Children (and adults) love it. It reminds me of a sort of homemade Spaghetti Hoops. Deliciously straightforward and comforting.

The potato is a simple, everyday thing, but it has a flavour that so often goes unappreciated. We treat it as a filler, or simply as starchy bulk on the side. When eaten like this, you appreciate its sweet, earthy qualities all over again.

In Sardinia, and in Nonna's family, this dish is eaten topped with a hard, salted cheese, which is made in a similar style to feta. If you like you can substitute feta, though any hard, salty cheese will work (ricotta salata, Lancashire, Parmesan or pecorino).

As this is such a simple recipe, it is important that even the smallest details are observed, such as the size and type of the potatoes. Nonna says she always finds that the yellower and firmer the potato, the better it is. And most often, she's right.

SERVES 4

500 g (1 lb 1¾ oz) waxy yellow potatoes, washed, peeled and diced into ½ cm (¼ in) pieces
½ small white onion, finely diced
1 stick of celery with leaves, diced very finely
5 tablespoons olive oil, plus extra for drizzling
a few sprigs of parsley (optional)
150 g (5¼ oz) tinned tomatoes, passed through a mouli or sieve, or passata
400 ml (14 fl oz/1¾ cups) Broth (page 185) or good-quality vegetable stock
1 Parmesan rind (if you have it; optional)
5 tablespoons small minestra pasta, such as ditalini, or broken lengths of spaghetti
sea salt
Parmesan, pecorino or cheese of your choice, to serve

In a saucepan over a medium heat, fry the diced potatoes, onion and celery in the olive oil until they are just beginning to colour, around 5–8 minutes, stirring all the time. Add the parsley and cook for a minute or two longer. Now add the tomatoes, broth and Parmesan rind (if using). Leave to simmer until the potatoes are completely tender, around 20 minutes.

Taste and check for salt. You want it to taste quite highly seasoned before you add the pasta, as it will absorb a lot of the salt. Drop in the pasta and cook until it is just al dente – the time will depend on your chosen pasta, so check the package for a rough time.

Serve in shallow bowls with some of your chosen cheese crumbled over, and an extra drizzle of good olive oil.

BROAD BEANS WITH GUANCIALE, VERNACCIA AND MINT

Fave con Pancetta, Vernaccia e Menta

The pairing of sweet, fresh broad (fava) beans and some form of salty bacon or ham is well-known and loved around the world.

In Sardinia, broad beans are braised with guanciale and served at room temperature as a delicious early summer *antipasto*. It is one of the nicest ways to enjoy them when in season.

Sometimes I add a torn tomato or two, sometimes not.

SERVES 6

2 tablespoons olive oil
1 garlic clove, bashed
60 g (2 oz) guanciale, diced
1.5 kg (3 lb 5 oz) broad (fava) beans, podded
100 ml (3⅓ oz/⅓ cup) vernaccia or another dry white wine
sea salt
handful of mint leaves, torn

Place the oil and garlic in a deep frying pan (skillet) over a medium heat. When the garlic begins to release its aroma, remove it and add the diced guanciale. Stir and cook until the guanciale begins to brown. Add the beans, a pinch of salt, the wine and 125 ml (4¼ fl oz/½ cup) water and braise for another 15–20 minutes, stirring occasionally, until the liquid has evaporated and the beans are totally tender and sweet.

Check the seasoning then serve with the torn mint leaves sprinkled over the top.

THE ART OF FRYING

Until I moved here, I never really appreciated fried food.

Of course I loved fish and chips, like a good Brit. I ate it perhaps once a year (rather through lack of opportunity than lack of desire) and I fried plenty of things when I worked in restaurants.

Then I moved to Sardinia. And I learnt about deep frying, the Sardinian way.

Here, deep frying is an art. And deep-fried food is eaten on a regular basis, so often that almost all the Sardinians I know have their own deep-fat fryers, and if they don't, then they have a gas hob set up outside on which to deep fry (without getting smoked out of the kitchen).

What amazed me - apart from the frequency of eating deep-fried food - was the quality and subtlety of it. Deep frying is done for a few reasons, primarily because everybody knows deep-fried food is delicious, but more importantly, because deep frying is one way to trap all the freshness, moisture, flavour and tenderness of a raw ingredient in. Deep frying here is not just a case of stodgy battered fish and soggy chips: deep-fried food in Sardinia is light, fresh, crisp, tender, moist and varied.

There are many nuances to deep-fat frying. There are different batters and coatings for different ingredients. There is deep-fat frying that involves *pastella* - or a batter, and there is deep-fat frying naked, where ingredients are simply dipped in flour, or egg and breadcrumbs. Like pasta and its corresponding sauces, it is horses for courses, and there is an appropriately crispy coating for every individual ingredient. The fried recipes I include in this book are only a tiny fraction of those that exist, but I hope they will tempt you to try it at home. If you follow the below advice there is no reason at all to fear frying.

First, the question of which oil to fry in. A contentious issue, as there are purists (like Nonna) who will only fry (whether shallow or deep) in olive oil. I like to deep fry battered things in flavourless oil, like sunflower or grape seed, because it is cheaper and does not impart any extra flavour.

When frying *nudo*, or with just a little dusting of flour, I like to fry in olive oil, as I think it tastes better. The Deep-fried peppers with anchovies and capers (page 88) are thus fried this way. Often I fry in a mix of the two, using part olive for flavour, and part sunflower for economy.

So that's the oil explained: now the batter. My batter recipe is very straightforward. The quantities stay the same, but the liquid is variable. Whether sparkling water, beer or prosecco, the fizziness ensures your finished fry is extra crispy.

In terms of temperature control, the easiest way if you are free-style frying (i.e. not using a deep-fat fryer) is to test the oil with a wooden spoon. As your oil heats dip in the handle of a wooden spoon; if the oil starts bubbling a little it is ready to fry with. If it bubbles aggressively and starts to smoke it is too hot, and the heat must be quickly turned down. If you are using a deep-fat fryer simply preheat it to 190°C (375°F).

The key to evenly golden, fried things is small batches, and a little space in between. This way your oil maintains a fairly even temperature.

If you are frying food for a lot
of people, put the oven on a low
setting and keep a baking (cookie)
sheet of the things that are ready
inside to keep warm whilst you
carry on.

Or, bite the bullet, embrace a life
of deliciously crispy fried things,
and buy yourself a little fryer.
I have friends in England who have
a deep-fat fryer at home and host

a weekly 'schnitzel and chips' night.
Rituals like these give you something
to look forward to. It is a sociable
way of cooking, too: when we're
frying, the guests tend to hover near
the fryer, and everyone snatches a hot
mouthful whilst chatting and drinking,
making things much more informal
and fun than offering fiddly canapes.

DEEP-FRIED PEPPERS WITH ANCHOVIES AND CAPERS

Peperoni Fritti con Acciughe e Capperi

I wasn't lying when I said the Sardinians love deep frying. Deep frying the peppers here means they become deliciously soft, silky and sweet, but you can achieve a similar result if you roast them slowly in the oven with lots of olive oil.

These are another of Franca's beloved antipasti, and they are addictively good. You can make them the day ahead and they are even better. In fact, they must sit for a few hours for the flavours to mellow and develop. The anchovy, vinegar and capers make a wonderfully piquant dressing to foil the sweetness.

Serve at room temperature, with plenty of crusty bread and some shards of salty pecorino cheese.

SERVES 4–6

500 ml (17 fl oz/2 cups) olive oil, for frying, plus extra for drizzling
3 large red peppers, deseeded and cut into eighths lengthways
8 anchovy fillets, torn lengthways
1 tablespoon capers
1 tablespoon red wine vinegar
sea salt
a few basil leaves, to serve

In a frying pan (skillet) over a medium heat, warm the olive oil and then fry the pieces of pepper until they are completely soft and just beginning to take colour. Remove and drain well on kitchen paper.

Heap the peppers into a mixing bowl and stir through the anchovies, capers and vinegar. Taste for seasoning. They shouldn't need salt as the anchovies are salty but if they are insipid, then add a pinch. Stir well and leave to sit for at least 1 hour – even better, 3–4 hours. Serve at room temperature, scattered with some fresh basil and drizzled with your best oil.

BAKED CARDONCELLI MUSHROOMS

Cardoncelli al Forno

This mushroom, which is foraged throughout the autumn and has a flavour and texture similar to an oyster mushroom, is best treated very simply, but precisely. Because of its especially high water content and propensity to be slimy (all mushrooms have this quality, but cardoncelli especially so), it is perfect for roasting whole in the oven with garlic, oil, plenty of salt and parsley. The edges become crisp and golden, and the centres soft and juicy. It makes a perfect lunch, alongside some fresh bread and a piece of pecorino.

In Sardinia, many households still have an outdoor wood-fired oven, and the flavour of these mushrooms is best coaxed out in this way.

SERVES 4

4 large cardoncelli mushrooms, or a mixture of oyster and chestnut (cremini) mushrooms
2 garlic cloves, finely sliced
a handful of parsley, roughly chopped
sea salt
extra virgin olive oil, for drizzling

Preheat the oven to 200°C (400°F/Gas 6).

Using a pastry brush, clean between the frills of the mushrooms, and wipe a damp piece of kitchen paper over them to remove any clinging dirt (don't wash them!).

Lightly oil an oven-proof dish and place the mushrooms flat-side down, with the stem facing upwards. Sprinkle the mushrooms with the garlic and parsley, a good pinch of salt, and drizzle them with the olive oil.

Place the dish in the oven and bake the mushrooms for about 20–30 minutes, or until they are well browned on the surface.

If you wish to make this more substantial you can add grated pecorino and/or breadcrumbs as a topping for your mushrooms.

CELERY AND BOTTARGA SALAD

Insalata di Sedano e Bottarga

This is one of those perfect (and rare) marriages where each component brings out the best in the other: crisp, cold and fresh celery, sliced and eaten alongside rich, bitter-sweet, fishy slithers of bottarga. I've served this dish to doubters – even those who have claimed to hate both celery and bottarga – and they are now converts.

It's a classic Sardinian salad, a perfect way to start a meal, and honestly, one of the nicest ways to enjoy celery. It is also delicious made with raw sliced artichokes.

SERVES 6 AS AN ANTIPASTO

2–3 heads of good-quality
    celery
1 lobe of bottarga
4 tablespoons best-quality
    olive oil
freshly cracked black pepper
crusty bread or pane carasau,
    to serve

Remove the outer, woodier stalks of the celery (save these for stock) and wash the crisper inside stalks well. Slice them into crescents about 3 mm thick. Slice the bottarga to roughly the same thickness. Arrange the celery on a serving platter and drizzle over the olive oil. Scatter the bottarga slices over the top and then crack some black pepper over the whole ensemble.

Eat with plenty of good crusty bread or pane carasau.

ARTICHOKE AND BOTTARGA SALAD

Insalata di Carciofi e bottarga

This is as good if not better than the Celery and bottarga salad (page 93), and just as simple to throw together, though the artichokes do need to be prepped (page 64).

SERVES 4 AS AN ANTIPASTO

6–8 fresh artichokes, prepped and kept
  in lemon water
juice of ½ a lemon
4 tablespoons best-quality olive oil
pinch of sea salt
½ head of radicchio or other coloured leaf
1 lobe of bottarga

Slice the prepped artichokes very thinly using a sharp knife and dress them immediately in the juice of the lemon and the oil. Add a pinch of salt and toss well. Mix in some shreds of radicchio for colour, then arrange on a serving platter. Slice the bottarga thinly and scatter over the top. Serve.

CELERY, BLOOD ORANGE, HAZELNUT AND PARMESAN

Insalata di Sedano, Arancia Sanguigna, Nocciole e Pecorino

One of the most refreshing and delicious seasonal winter salads in the world, you can almost feel your insides thanking you.

SERVES 4 AS A STARTER OR SIDE DISH

70 g (2½ oz) hazelnuts
2 heads of celery
2 blood oranges
6 tablespoons best-quality olive oil,
  plus extra to serve
pinch of sea salt
zest and juice of 1 small orange
juice of ½ a lemon
50 g (1¾ oz) Parmesan, shaved

Preheat the oven to 170°C (340°F/Gas 3).
    Roast the hazelnuts on a baking (cookie) sheet for around 8 minutes, until just golden. Set aside.
    Remove the tougher, outer stalks of the celery and wash the inside stalks well. Keep the inner paler leaves attached to the stalk – these are good to eat. Slice each stalk on the diagonal to get slightly elongated crescents.
    Cut away the pith and peel from the blood oranges and cut them into chunks roughly the same size as the celery.
    In a bowl, mix the celery with the oil, salt, citrus juice and zest and toss well with your hands.
    Arrange the dressed celery on a serving platter and dot the orange chunks over the top. Sprinkle over the shavings of Parmesan and the hazelnuts, slightly crushed in your hands. Drizzle with extra oil and serve.

PERSIMMON, PROSCIUTTO, ENDIVES, PECORINO AND WALNUTS

Cachi, Indivia, Pecorino e Noci

A delicious combination of things that all happen to come into season here in late autumn.

The kind of persimmons most often grown here are the hachiya, which become so soft when ripe that they collapse at the touch of a finger. The flavour is hard to describe: a little honey, a little vanilla, a lot of sweetness. They cry out for acidity. Here, they are paired with some salt, some bitterness and some crunch. The orange juice and zest in the dressing brings out the best in the persimmon.

SERVES 4–6

2½ tablespoons olive oil
zest and juice of 1 orange
juice 1 lemon
pinch of sea salt
2 ripe persimmons
2 heads endive or other
   bitter leaf, such as radicchio,
   or a combination
4–6 slices prosciutto
1 handful of walnuts

Make a dressing by whisking the oil, citrus juices, zest and salt.

Scoop out the flesh of the persimmons and arrange them in amber blobs on a serving plate. Dress the leaves in a large bowl with most of the dressing and tumble them over the persimmon. Drizzle extra dressing on the persimmon, lay over the slices of prosciutto and scatter over the walnuts. Serve.

photo overleaf →

CASU

On an island where sheep outnumber people three to one, it is perhaps unsurprising that sheeps' milk cheeses are one of Sardinia's most famous and ancient products. Ewe's milk cheeses have been made here since prehistoric times.

Little has changed in Sardinian cheese-making. Some milking is now mechanised, though many still choose to do it by hand. All sheep roam the hills free-range, and the cheese-making is usually done using traditional wooden tools.

There are millions of cheeses made on the island, from cow's, sheep's and goat's milk. However, Sardinia is best known for pecorino, a hard sheeps' milk cheese that is split into three main varieties: pecorino Sardo, pecorino Romano and fiore Sardo. Pecorino Sardo can be eaten young or matured and has a sweet richness and depth, similar to aged Parmesan. This is the cheese I use in most of my recipes. Pecorino Romano (which is also made in Lazio) is stronger, saltier and spicier. Fiore Sardo (which is said to date back to the Bronze Age) is one of Sardinia's most ancient cheeses and is smoked over herbs, rendering it with a darker rind and a strong, fruity and smoky flavour. Some of the world's most unusual cheeses are also made here, in particular, *casu mazu*, but it's an acquired taste. The name translates as 'rotten cheese', which will give some indication of the flavour. This cheese is made by encouraging a particular fly (the cheese fly) to lay eggs in a traditional pecorino, and then leaving it in a protected environment until the eggs hatch into maggots. The maggots then eat and 'pass' the cheese, creating a soft, acidic, semi-digested cheese that Sardinians prize. Though this cheese has been made illegal for human consumption, it is widely eaten

nonetheless. Sardinians believe it is full of good things, and many attribute their long lives to the regular consumption of it.

The Romans made and ate a great deal of cheese. Apparently they also believed it 'increased fertility and fostered love-making'. Whether it arouses you or not, there is no denying that cheese is a magical foodstuff. It is true alchemy in the way that it relies on a third party (the mysterious mould) to work magic and create its unique flavour. However controlled you are in your production environment, no two cheeses will ever taste exactly the same. There are so many contributing factors that give it its unique flavour, from the type of milk to the diet of the cow, sheep or goat, to the time of the year that it is made.

In terms of cookery, specifically Sardinian cookery, cheese is the cook's greatest gift, after olive oil, wine and wheat. Almost every Sardinian dish contains some or other form of cheese, whether it be savoury or sweet. Unlike many Italians, the Sards have no qualms about eating cheese with fish.

Pecorino is one of Sardinia's principle exports. Here it is eaten in great craggy slabs, sometimes before the meal as an antipasto, or after the meal, and generally throughout the day. There is no time of day when pecorino seems inappropriate. A good pecorino (depending on its age) can rival a fine Parmesan, and should have the same rich nuttiness, but with the addition of a distinctive, sheepy background note. There are a few recipes that require the use of both (numerous pesto recipes, for example) and I think the combination of the two is hard to beat.

FIGS, SPECK, BITTER LEAVES AND RICOTTA SALATA

Fichi, Speck, Radicchio e Ricotta Salata

Let us be clear here: most Sardinians do not put fruit in salads. Their puritanical attitude to food means their salad components barely even extend to lemon juice or vinegar. A salad in Sardinia generally means green lettuce dressed only with olive oil and salt. It's delicious – the oil is so good it couldn't fail to be.

But then, as I said in the introduction to this book, cookery is full of contradictions. Recipes are made by people, and people are contrary beings. Sards love to pair the salt of cured hams with the sweet clarity of melon, or the sun-ripe jamminess of figs. Here, I have taken this idea and spun it out into an ensemble salad.

I love to eat fruit in salads, and I have made such sweet-savoury combinations often, and they are (mostly) well received, despite a few rumblings about the English being 'strange' and all our food being 'confused', which are par for the course. This salad is a celebration of some of the best ingredients, and one of my favourite things to eat when the figs are ripe. *Vive la révolution!*

SERVES 4–6

juice and zest of 1 small lemon
good pinch of sea salt
1 teaspoon honey
6 tablespoons best-quality
    extra virgin olive oil, to serve
6 ripe black figs
1 head radicchio or other
    bitter leaf, leaves separated
1 bunch of rocket or small
    green leaf of your choice
60 g (2 oz) ricotta salata, shaved
6 slices of speck or prosciutto

Make a rough dressing by mixing the lemon juice and zest, salt, honey and olive oil.

Rip open the figs and arrange them on a serving platter. Dress the leaves well and arrange them over the figs. Scatter over the ricotta and dot the speck slices around. Drizzle with extra oil and serve.

GREEN BEAN, POTATO, OLIVE, TUNA, TOMATO AND BASIL SALAD

Insalata Estiva di Fagiolini, Patate, Olive, Tonno, Basilico e Pomodori

A sort of Sardinian Niçoise, and a celebration of late summer. Tuna is delicious, though if you would like to make it a little more colourful, you can use prawns (shrimp) instead.

Perfect for a simple summer lunch, with a glass or two of Vermentino.

Make sure you cook the beans until completely tender in well-salted water – this is not a place for squeaky beans.

SERVES 4

200 g (7 oz) new potatoes,
    cooked, cooled and peeled,
    or unpeeled
4 large, ripe tomatoes
½ garlic clove
pinch of sea salt
3 tablespoons red wine vinegar
8 tablespoons best-quality
    olive oil
200 g (7 oz) green beans,
    cooked in salted water
    and cooled
handful of olives (of your choice)
200 g (7 oz) tuna or cooked
    prawns (shrimp)
handful of basil leaves

Cut the potatoes and the tomatoes into even sized pieces, slices or chunks, whichever you feel like.

Mince the clove of garlic and mix with the salt and the vinegar and oil to make a rough dressing.

Place the potatoes, tomatoes, beans, olives and fish in a mixing bowl. Tear half the basil leaves over, and add the dressing. Mix well, with your hands. Lay out on a serving platter and serve with the rest of the fresh basil torn over the top.

FOUR

GRANO

Pear, Pecorino and Ricotta Ravioli • Pumpkin, Ricotta and Chilli Ravioli with Brown Butter and Sage • *The Taste of Sunshine and Earth* • Linguine with Bottarga and Clams • Spaghetti with Bottarga Two Ways • Malloredus with Sausage Ragù • Malloreddus with Mutton Broth and Pecorino • Lina's Culurgionis • *A Sauce for All Seasons* • Tomato Sauce Three Ways • Linguine with Lemon, Basil, Pecorino and Mascarpone • Trofie with Pesto, Tuna and Tomatoes • Pasta with Butter to Save and Salve • Red Wine and Radicchio Risotto with Sapa • Fregola with Clams and Fennel • Saffron, Orange and Mascarpone Risotto • Perfect Polenta • Polenta, Sausage, Cheese and Tomato Bake • *At Best Ignored, at Worst a Nuisance* • Chickpeas with Wild Fennel and Ham • Brown Lentil, Sage and Chestnut Soup with Ricotta • Eggs in Tomato Sauce with Music Paper Bread

GRANO

Grains of various types have always formed an important part of Mediterranean cuisine. They provide essential nutrients and energy and are a staple of every peasant diet. Sardinia has a rich tradition of specialist pastas and grains, which are often cited as one the major reasons the island's inhabitants are so long-lived.

One of the most important products in Sardinia is *semola*: a product of hard durum wheat ground to a sandy 'flour' that we in England would call semolina. Durum wheat is a type of hard-wheat that is cultivated all over Italy, including Sardinia, due to its 'hard' nature, during milling, its starchy endosperm (which is yellow – thus giving pasta its golden colour) remains intact. This is used to make almost all the various types of pasta consumed on the island. Unlike some areas of Italy, here it is unusual to find pasta made from finely ground soft wheat (00) flour and fresh eggs. The fresh pastas are usually based around the simple semola and water dough (page 128). Again, this is an inheritance of poverty, as eggs were considered too expensive. I rarely make fresh egg pasta as I find it very rich, but there are certain occasions when it suits the sauce so well it is worth it (page 112). I eat much more dried pasta because it is versatile, cheap, and I prefer the texture. Dried pasta is a staple of the Sardinian diet. Good dried pasta is made purely from durum wheat. All dried pasta should be made from this type of wheat, which, once milled, is also known as *semola di gran duro*. This is high in protein, and has a lower glycaemic index than softer wheat varieties. It also makes the best pasta, as it is high in starch, so the pasta does not stick together when cooking, and the flavour is superior.

Fregola is one of Sardinia's most quintessential and iconic pastas. It is made by rolling small pellet-like balls out of a durum wheat semolina and water dough. These pellets are then lightly roasted in an oven, which imparts a delicious toasty flavour to the pasta, and gives it its trademark variation of sandy brown colours.

The true origins of fregola are unknown, though it is thought the Sardinians may have inherited the method from the North African production of couscous.

RICE AND PULSES

Rice grows well in Sardinia, and is almost always cooked in a similar way to cooking risotto; starting sautéed with perhaps butter or oil and a little onion, and then liquid added slowly whilst stirring to make sure the rice absorbs it.

Polenta (cornmeal) is another grain-based ingredient that you'll find in most Sardinian kitchens. It has a bad reputation, but undeservedly so. It can be blindingly bland, or gloriously good, depending on how it is treated. I have a deep, deep love for polenta. It is cheap, filling and the ultimate comfort food.

Finally, lentils and beans proliferate in Sardinian cuisine. Dried broad (fava) beans are a staple throughout the winter, cannellini, and fresh and dried borlotti (cranberry beans) appear frequently too. Chickpeas (garbanzo beans) form the body of nourishing bowlfuls in the colder months.

NOTE

Any remaining filling can be
frozen and used another time.

110

PEAR, PECORINO AND RICOTTA RAVIOLI

Ravioli di Pera, Pecorino e Ricotta

Based on a brilliant recipe by Emiko Davies, these are surprisingly delicate and dainty ravioli that will win over any sweet-with-savoury sceptic.

The filling can be made well in advance and kept in the fridge for a few days.

The ravioli are very good served simply with olive oil, fresh basil (in summer) and a little extra cheese, but they are even better in winter served with some toasted walnuts and sage butter. The filling can be made well in advance and kept in the fridge for a few days.

For the sage butter, see page 112.

SERVES 6

3 pears, peeled, cored
    and halved
1 tablespoon brown sugar
peeled zest of ½ a lemon
350 g (12⅓ oz) ricotta
100 g (3½ oz) pecorino, grated,
    plus extra to serve
sea salt
1 x quantity Fresh egg pasta
    dough (page 112)
semolina, for dusting
sage butter (page 112)
a handful walnuts, toasted

In a small saucepan, poach the pears gently in a little water with the sugar and lemon until they are just soft, about 10 minutes. Allow to cool, then slice them into tiny pieces, about the size of a petit pois.

In a small bowl, mix the pear with the ricotta, pecorino and a good pinch of sea salt, then taste for seasoning. The mix needs to be well seasoned, because ricotta drinks salt.

Cut the pasta into 4 pieces and roll each into a long thick strip using a pasta machine, or a rolling pin, until it is thin enough to just see your hand through. Keep dusting your surfaces with semolina to prevent sticking. Dust a tray with semolina ready to place your ravioli onto.

Using a piping bag or a teaspoon, dot walnut-sized amounts of your filling 5 cm (2 in) apart, in the centre of your wide strip of pasta. Cut each into a strip containing just 3 of your ravioli. Lightly brush the lower half with a little water and fold over the top half of the pasta sheet to enclose the filling. Press down gently using the palms of your hands and seal the ravioli all the way around. Cut them out into squares or half-moons, depending on your preference. Place on the tray and chill for 30 minutes.

When ready to cook, bring a large pan of well-salted water to the boil, and have the sage butter ready to go in a frying pan (skillet) big enough to accommodate all the ravioli. Drop in your ravioli and cook them for 3–4 minutes, until they bob to the surface and the pasta is cooked through.

Decant them with a slotted spoon into the sage butter, stir gently to coat and serve, with toasted walnuts and more grated pecorino on top.

PUMPKIN, RICOTTA AND CHILLI RAVIOLI WITH BROWN BUTTER AND SAGE

Ravioli di Zucca e Ricotta con Burro Caramellato e Salvia

One of the few occasions I make fresh egg pasta, but very much worth the effort. The sweet, earthy, vivid-orange filling is pure comfort. If you wanted to gild the lily further you could add some toasted hazelnuts or walnuts on top.

Whilst this is one of the more involved recipes in the book, the ravioli freeze brilliantly, and if you make a large batch you can whip out a few every time you have unexpected guests.

SERVES 6

250 g (8¾ oz/generous 2 cups) 00 flour
3 medium egg yolks
2 medium whole eggs

For the filling

1 large pumpkin (I like to use onion squash), peeled and cut into wedges
sea salt
2 dried chillies, crushed, or 1 scant teaspoon chilli flakes
6 tablespoons olive oil
zest of 1 lemon
250 g (9 oz) ricotta
80 g (3 oz) Parmesan, grated
1 x quantity pasta dough (see above)
semolina, for dusting

For the sauce

150 g (5¼ oz) butter
8–10 sage leaves
40 g (1½ oz) Parmesan, grated, plus extra to serve

To make the pasta dough, mix the ingredients together, either by hand, with a spoon or in a mixer. Knead well (a good 10 minutes here) until you have a smooth, even dough. Wrap in cling film (plastic wrap) and leave to rest for a good 30 minutes.

Preheat the oven to 180°C (350°F/Gas 4).

In a roasting tin, season the pumpkin well with a pinch of salt, chilli and olive oil. Roast in the oven until soft and caramelised, about 40–50 minutes. Leave to cool completely.

Mash the cooked pumpkin in a bowl with a fork and add the lemon zest, ricotta and Parmesan. Taste for seasoning. You may like to add more chilli at this point, too.

Set aside to cool completely, either at room temperature or in the fridge.

Cut the pasta dough in half, then, using a machine, roll the dough (adding flour when necessary) until it's thin enough to just see your hand through, then lay out one strip on a floured surface. Take walnut-sized pieces of the filling and place in the centre of the pasta at 5 cm (2 in) intervals. Dampen the pasta sheet with a pastry brush dipped in water and fold the top part of the sheet over the bottom, pressing down with your fingers to seal. Cut the ravioli and place on a tray well coated in semolina. Put in the fridge to chill until you want to serve them.

You'll need to make the sauce at the same time as cooking the pasta. Melt the butter in a shallow pan over a medium heat, add the sage leaves and continue cooking it, letting it bubble away until it just begins to turn brown.

As you melt the butter for the sauce, bring a large pan of salted water to the boil. Drop in the ravioli and cook for 2–3 minutes, until they bob to the surface.

Once the butter for the sauce has begun to brown, add a ladle of the pasta cooking water and turn down the heat, stirring. Add the Parmesan and stir over a low heat until an emulsion is formed.

Remove the pasta from the water with a slotted spoon and place in the sauce. Serve with a sprinkling of Parmesan on top.

NOTE
Any remaining filling can be frozen and used another time.

THE TASTE OF
SUNSHINE AND EARTH

The Italian attitude to pasta epitomises the passion for their cuisine in general: a humble ingredient is treated with love, cooked with infinite care, and thus elevated to something truly special. Luca summed it up in his inimitable way when he cooked a plate of *pasta al pomodoro* recently. We were in a rush and he made the sauce quickly. As he brought me my plate born aloft in a single hand he said: 'Ehhh Letiiiiizia - just so you know - I make this with the 'and, not with the 'art!'. Pasta in Italy is (almost) always made with the heart.

Pasta is not only cheap, delicious, quick to cook and easy to prepare, it is also, by the very nature of its form, a fun foodstuff. There is no other food as joyful. Each shape is an art-form and a celebration in itself, whether it's a bow-tie and a butterfly (*farfalle*), a shell (*conchiglie*), a snail (*lumache*), tiny ears (*orecchiette*) or radiators (*radiatori*). Pasta, in all its various shapes and sizes, is a testament to ingenuity, creativity and skill. Italy has between 350-500 different shapes of pasta, from the sublime (*su filindeu* - 'threads of God') to the ridiculous (novelty penis-shaped pasta available at every Italian tourist hotspot).

In Sardinia, and in Italy in general, the pasta is as important as the sauce. Pasta is not merely a vehicle - it is an essential part of the finished dish. The perfect amount of sauce should allow you to taste both the pasta and the sauce. I am always amazed when people say that pasta is just a filler and has no flavour. It is like saying bread has no flavour. Pasta tastes of the mellow gold of wheat, of bread, of grain. It tastes of sunshine and earth.

To cook pasta, you must have a large, deep pan full of boiling water as 'salty as the sea'. I cook pasta approximately 2 minutes less than the advised time on the packet to achieve my perfect *al dente*. There should be a good bite to it, but it must not taste raw or floury. Practise will show you how to judge this. A small cup of cooking water must be reserved once the pasta is cooked. The sauce must be made separately, and warmed in a roomy pan large enough to hold pasta and sauce with space to spare. The drained pasta is then added to the sauce and tossed vigorously over the heat, with some of the reserved cooking water added. Carry on cooking, tossing and tasting until the sauce amalgamates and the pasta is coated and juicy, rather than dry or swimming in sauce. I have known chefs who swear that the pasta must be tossed at least 20 times. You will see when the pasta is saucy but not swimming, when the sauce is loose but not runny, when the whole lot looks *complete* somehow. Nonna says the pasta is not ready until it *squelches*, a suggestive sound which always makes her chuckle.

Cooking pasta al dente is a national institution in Italy, though it will vary wildly from region to region and from household to household. Luca's family will have long arguments on the subject. Giuseppe, Luca's father, will frequently push a plate of '*stracotto*' (overcooked) pasta away in disgust if Franca has absent-mindedly left it a few seconds too long in the water, but will also complain of Luca's more al dente pasta being '*duro*' (hard). The perfect al dente is relative, and human nature being as contrary as it is means that there is really no such thing as perfectly al dente pasta. But

there is definitely an area of correctness between the stracotto and the duro, and only frequent experimentation and tasting will allow you to find this.

In Italy it is not uncommon to be asked how much pasta you would like to eat in grams. What is often seen as a disadvantage of pasta (the fact that it makes you feel bloated or heavy) is due to mistakes with portioning. A large portion of pasta will make anyone feel bloated and heavy. I aim for 80-100 g (3-3½ oz) of pasta per person, per portion. More like 80 g (3 oz) if it's a *primi*, and 100 g (3½ oz) if it's a *secondo*. If I'm hungover, I cook 250-300 g (9-10½ oz) for myself, though I am aware of the consequences.

LINGUINE WITH BOTTARGA AND CLAMS

Linguine con Bottarga e Arselle

This would probably be my Desert Island Dish. I didn't think linguine with clams could ever be improved upon, until I met its fishier, feistier Sardinian relative.

The first time I ever tried *Spaghetti alla Vongole* (traditionally clams are always served with either linguine or spaghetti) was when I was a student back in Venice, and I remember a large, steaming, oval platter arriving and being placed in the centre of the table. There was a great, pale mound of spaghetti, some flecks of chilli and parsley; pebble-like clams scattered here and there. The waiter picked up two forks and proceeded to twirl, lift and portion the pasta, with the dramatic ceremony only Italian waiters can command, the clams tinkling as they landed on our expectant plates.

It smelled wonderful, but to my English eyes, it looked a little lacking in 'sauce'. Then I tried a mouthful, and realised that the sweet, winy and briny juice of clams, perfumed with garlic and spiked with a little chilli, is the most heavenly sauce there is. The Sardinian version celebrates this, and enhances it with bottarga.

Bottarga, like bacon or Parmesan, is a way of enhancing and enrichening delicious, savoury, umami flavours. It works like a fishy version of Parmesan; just as you add grated cheese to many meat or vegetable-based pasta sauces, so you add grated bottarga to fish-based ones.

The portion here is for a main – this is just too good to eat as a *primo* in small quantities, to my mind at least.

SERVES 4

400 g (14 oz) linguine
10 tablespoons best-quality olive oil
2 garlic cloves, halved
healthy pinch of dried chilli flakes
800 g (1 lb 12 oz) clams, cleaned, open or broken shells removed
90 ml 3 fl oz/⅓ cup) white wine
handful of flat leaf parsley, roughly chopped
3 tablespoons freshly grated bottarga
sea salt

Bring a large pan of well-salted water to the boil. Drop in your linguine.

Meanwhile, pour half the olive oil into another wide pan. Place over a medium heat and add the halves of garlic. When the garlic just begins to sizzle and smell good, add the chilli and tip in your clams. Stir to coat the clams with oil then add your wine, turn the heat to high and put a lid on the whole pan. Wait a minute, shaking the pan occasionally, then remove the lid and turn the heat to medium and allow the sauce to simmer away and reduce a little.

Now drain the pasta (it should be nicely *al dente*) reserving a small cup of cooking liquid.

Add the parsley, a little cooking liquid and the rest of the olive oil to the clams. Stir vigorously, tossing and shaking the pan to emulsify the sauce. If it starts to look too dry, add some more of your reserved cooking liquid.

Finally, add the grated bottarga and shake and stir vigorously again, emulsifying the whole lot into a creamy sauce.

Serve with a glass of chilled white wine.

NOTE

In theory the clam sauce is the work of moments, but if you are nervous
of making it in the time it takes for the pasta to cook it can be made before
and set aside away from the heat. Clams are quite forgiving and can wait
10 minutes or so (in their juice) whilst you diligently monitor your pasta.
When the pasta is perfectly al dente, you can mix the two and the pasta
will warm through the clams sufficiently. I often do it this way, too.

SPAGHETTI WITH BOTTARGA TWO WAYS

Spaghetti alla Bottarga

There are as many ways to make *spaghetti alla bottarga* as there are cooks in Sardinia. Some feel anything more than half a clove of garlic and some good oil is overkill – unsurprisingly Luca is firmly in this camp – whilst others like to add butter, black pepper or tomatoes.

To me there is no bad version, and if you like both bottarga and spaghetti you will like them any which way. However, the recipes opposite are two of my favourites.

SPAGHETTI WITH BOTTARGA AND TOMATOES

Spaghetti alla Bottarga con Pomodorini

SERVES 4

200 g (7 oz) pomodorini (small sweet tomatoes
   such as cherry or datterini)
2 garlic cloves, finely chopped
1 dried red chilli
4 tablespoons best-quality extra virgin olive oil,
   plus extra to serve
sea salt
400 g (14 oz) spaghetti
a handful of chopped parsley
100 g (3½ oz) bottarga, finely grated,
   plus extra to serve

Cut the tomatoes in half and squeeze out the majority
of the seeds, then discard them. Tip into a bowl with
the chopped garlic, dried chilli, oil and a pinch of salt.
Leave to infuse for around 20 minutes.

   Bring a large saucepan of salted water to the boil.
Drop in your spaghetti.

   Warm the tomatoes in a pan large enough to contain
everything. Drain the pasta and add it to the tomatoes.
Add the chopped parsley and stir and toss vigorously.
Now add the bottarga and continue stirring and tossing
until you have a good thick sauce. Serve with extra grated
bottarga on top, and a drizzle of oil.

SPAGHETTI WITH BOTTARGA, GARLIC AND CHILLI

Spaghetti alla Bottarga con Aglio e Peperoncino

As this is such an incredibly simple dish, it is
more important than ever that the pasta is very
al dente. Sardinians claim it helps to balance
the richness of the bottarga, and they are right.
The faint crunchiness of the pasta is essential.

SERVES 2

200 g (7 oz) spaghetti
3 tablespoons olive oil,
   plus best-quality oil for drizzling
1 garlic clove, halved
1 small dried red chilli
50 g (1¾ oz) bottarga, finely grated
sea salt

Bring a large pan of salted water to the boil. Drop in
your spaghetti.

   Meanwhile, in your favourite wide pasta pan, heat
the oil and garlic until the garlic just begins to sizzle and
take colour. Take off the heat, add the chilli and set aside.

   Drain your spaghetti (reserving a little of the cooking
liquid) and throw it into the pan with the oil, chilli and
garlic. Place the pan over a low heat and add the bottarga,
a splash or two of your reserved pasta cooking liquid and
an extra drizzle of your best oil.

   Toss and stir well, until you have a good saucy
consistency. Serve.

MALLOREDUS WITH SAUSAGE RAGÙ

Malloreddus alla Campidanese

This is one of Sardinia's most iconic dishes. Malloreddus are small, ridged pasta nuggets, still made by hand in many parts of Sardinia, and known also as Sardinian gnocchi.

They are made with a simple two parts semolina, one part water mix. It is traditional to add a pinch of saffron to give the dough a beautiful yellow hue, as though it had been made with good eggs; a tradition inherited from a time when eggs were more expensive in Sardinia than saffron. These are so easy to make it will banish any fear of making pasta at home that you have ever had, and the fact that they require nothing fresh, only some flour forgotten at the back of the cupboard, and water from a tap, makes them a brilliant fall-back for an empty fridge. The dough is pliable and forgiving to work with, and even better, you do not need a pasta machine.

The traditional shape of the malloreddus is formed by rolling one side of the nuggets along a Sardinian wicker basket, though many now use a gnocchi board. If you cannot find either, then the tines of a fork will do fine. The ridges are necessary and important as they are designed to catch and trap the thick sauce.

The sauce is named after the large plain of Campidano, and is the Sardinian equivalent of the beloved Bolognaise ragù.

Like all good ragùs, it is satisfying, savoury and rich. Fat is flavour, and here the depth of the sauce is provided by a good, fatty sausage. The tomatoes cook slowly into sweet and slippery submission, whilst the saffron and chilli provide welcome notes of heat and spice.

I am not, as a rule, a great fan of sausages. I rarely cook them. Mostly because I find lots of them pale, flabby and flavourless. A good sausage should be almost the same colour as salami, dark and rich and visibly composed of chunks of real meat and fat, in equal proportions. In Sardinia, the sausages are generally much meatier.

Try to find the best sausages you can – really, properly meaty and fatty at the same time. Toulouse or Tuscan are good options.

SERVES 6

For the malloreddus

300 g (10½ oz/2 cups) fine semolina, plus extra for dusting
pinch of sea salt
pinch of saffron powder

Mix all the ingredients together with 150 ml (5 fl oz/⅔ cup) water and work (either with your hands or in an electric mixer) until you have a nice smooth dough. Leave to rest under a cloth for 30 minutes – I usually use the time to clear up.

Cut the dough into 5 even pieces and roll them into long sausages around 1 cm (½ in) width, then cut each piece of dough into 1 cm- (½ in-) square nuggets.

If things are getting soft or sticky, add more semolina.

Take each little nugget and press it down in the middle and roll it down the back of a fork, or on your gnocchi board. Place on a tray sprinkled with semolina.

At this point you can use them straight away or they can be kept in the fridge for a day or two, or frozen for up to a month.

If you wish to, you can dry them out completely in the sun or in a very low oven then store in an airtight container indefinitely.

For the sauce

1 large white onion, diced
2 garlic cloves, sliced
4 tablespoons olive oil
4 fresh bay leaves
1 small dried chilli
pinch of saffron powder
300 g (10½ oz) sausage meat
2 x 400 g (14 oz) tins tomatoes
100 ml (3½ fl oz/scant ½ cup)
   white wine, ideally vernaccia
sea salt
150 g (5¼ oz) pecorino, grated,
   plus extra to serve
parsley, finely chopped,
   to serve

To make the sauce, cook the onion and garlic in the oil in a wide, deep pan over a medium heat until soft and beginning to brown, around 10 minutes. Add the bay leaf, chilli, saffron, sausagemeat, making sure to break it up into small pieces. Continue to fry and stir over a medium heat until the sausage is cooked and golden. Add the tomatoes, wine and a small splash of water, and leave to simmer for at least 40 minutes. Keep stirring whenever you think of it and continue mushing up the sausage with your spoon. Taste and check for seasoning.

Bring another pan of water to the boil and salt well. Tip in your malloreddus and cook for 1–2 minutes, until they bob to the surface. Ladle out and place in the hot sauce with a small ladle of pasta cooking water. Add the grated pecorino and stir gently, turning all of the nuggets over in their sauce. Continue to cook for another minute or so until the sauce turns silky.

Spoon into shallow bowls and serve with more grated pecorino, if you wish, and parsley.

MALLOREDDUS WITH MUTTON BROTH AND PECORINO

Malloreddus con Pecora e Pecorino

If there is one dish that sums up Sardinia for me, it is this – an ode to sheep. Simplicity itself, the dish requires just three ingredients: mutton stock, pasta and cheese.

This is a speciality of the Nuoro region, and I first ate it here cooked by a local shepherd, Fabrizio, who looked as though he'd popped straight out of the Bible. He had killed one of his own sheep especially. He'd made the pecorino too. It was and is still, one of the best – and the most humble – meals I have ever had.

Traditionally, the pasta is followed by the Poached mutton and vegetables, which appears on page 182. If you cannot find mutton (though good butchers will still sell it) then I suggest you use a really flavoursome cut of lamb, such as neck. If you can find hogget (a middle-aged animal) that is also good.

This is an unusual pasta recipe in that it is cooked like a risotto. The broth is added slowly, ladle by ladle, whilst the pasta cooks and absorbs the liquid. It is surprisingly easy and effective, as you have complete control over how saucy your finished pasta will be.

SERVES 3–4

For the stock

1.5 kg (3 lb 5 oz) mutton,
   lamb neck or hogget
3–4 litres (101–135 fl oz/
   12–17 cups) cold water

For the pasta

1.2 litres (41 fl oz/5 cups)
   mutton stock
300 g (10½ oz) malloreddus
   (page 122)
sea salt
300 g (10½ oz) mixed
   grated cheese (a mixture
   of Parmesan, aged and
   fresh pecorino is best)
freshly ground black pepper

First make your stock. This can be done up to 4 days in advance and then kept in the fridge or freezer. Place the meat in a large stock pot and cover with the cold water. Bring to a low simmer and skim away any scum that rises to the surface. Cook for anything from 2–3 hours; until the meat is tender and giving.

Ladle off the quantity of stock needed for cooking your pasta. The rest of the stock, along with the poached meat will be used for the recipe on page 182, so once cool, store in an airtight container in the fridge until ready to use.

In your best, deep and wide pasta or risotto pan, spoon in a few ladles of stock and place over a gentle heat. Add the pasta and stir occasionally.

Meanwhile, between stirs, finely grate your cheese.

Continue adding ladles of stock and stirring gently until it is absorbed, just as though you were cooking a risotto. It should take around 12–15 minutes for your pasta to be perfectly al dente.

Taste and check you are happy with the texture (you may also wish to add a small pinch of salt here). When it is as *al dente* as you wish, add the grated cheese and any remaining stock. Stir well until a lovely, thick and melty cheese sauce has formed; if you have used all your stock you can add a little water.

Serve with some freshly ground black pepper on top.

LINA'S CULURGIONIS

It is hard not to fall for these rustic, chubby, Sardinian cousins of ravioli. More like dumplings, they are made of a simple semolina pasta dough stuffed with a filling of cheese, garlic, potato and mint, and shaped into an oval parcel with a plaited seam formed by a series of deft nips and tucks. The Sardinians say they resemble an ear of wheat. Like ravioli, culurgionis are poached in salted boiling water for a few minutes and served with tomato sauce and grated pecorino, or occasionally sage butter.

Lina makes the best culurgionis of anyone we know. Her family come from the Ogliastra region of Sardinia, where culurgionis originated. The first time I ate them she brought them as a gift, presenting the podgy parcels in a pizza box to protect them, each one shaped by hand and tucked into a miniature paper case like a luxurious bon bon. As she lifted the lid of the box there was a great gasp, as all those present admired the perfect little plaited pouches.

They were as delicious as they looked: chewy, cheesy and utterly homely in flavour. Aside from their taste and appearance, there is something squidgy and appealing about their name – the Sards pronounce them '*curr-low-joe-nee*', which means 'little bundles'.

These are quite intricate to make, so I would recommend saving them for a special occasion. However, four or five per person is ample, so if you make them for an intimate dinner *à deux*, you only have to make ten, which isn't too time-demanding.

The cheese can be varied according to what you have available, but this is Lina's magic combination. She also adds an egg to her filling, which is unusual, but seems to make it lighter and fluffier.

SERVES 6–8

For the filling

700 g (1 lb 8¾ oz) yellow
  potatoes
3 tablespoons olive oil
1 egg
1 small garlic clove, grated
100 g (3½ oz) pecorino, finely
  grated, plus extra to serve
80 g (2¾ oz) Parmesan, finely
  grated, plus extra to serve
70 g (2½ oz) Provoletta, other
  mild soft cow's cheese
  or cheddar, finely grated
handful of mint leaves,
  finely chopped
sea salt, to taste

For the dough

300 g (10½ oz/1¾ cups)
  semolina
1 tablespoon olive oil
pinch of sea salt

To serve

1 x quantity tomato sauce
  of your choice (page 135)
basil leaves, to serve

First, make the filling. Drop the potatoes into a saucepan of well-salted water and bring to the boil. When the potatoes are cooked through, drain well and peel them with your fingers (much easier when they are warm) and pass them through a ricer or mouli. Mix with the oil, egg, garlic, cheese and mint. Mix together well (I find this easiest with my hands) and taste for seasoning. Add salt if necessary. Cover and place in the fridge for at least 30 minutes, or long enough to cool, but you can also make it the night before and leave overnight, if you like.

Next, make the dough. Mix all of the ingredients with 140 ml (4¾ fl oz/⅔ cup) water using your hands or a stand mixer and knead until you have a smooth, even dough; this will take at least 5 minutes of good, firm kneading. Wrap in cling film (plastic wrap) and leave to rest for half an hour. Again, you can do this the night before.

Roll out the dough with a pasta machine or a rolling pin, adding flour when necessary, until it is 1–2 mm or so thick. Use a highball glass to cut circles from the dough. Take a walnut-sized piece of the filling, shape it smoothly and place it in the centre of the dough. Using your left hand to cup it, fold and pleat the dough over itself to encase the filling, as shown on page 126. Place on a tray and set aside.

Once made, these will keep for about 4 days in the fridge and freeze well.

When ready to cook, bring a large pan of salted water to the boil. Drop in the culurgionis and cook for 2–3 minutes until they rise to the surface. Remove with a slotted spoon and place into a warm sauce. Stir to coat and serve with basil leaves and cheese.

A SAUCE FOR
ALL SEASONS

SUGO AL POMODORO

Tomato sauce is one of the cornerstones of Italian cooking. It is served with meat, with pasta, with ravioli, with polenta, with sausages, with fish. The hallowed status of this sauce is no doubt due to its adaptability, economy and dependable deliciousness.

A good tomato sauce is a simple thing, but that does not mean it is simple to achieve. It takes care to create something so simple and yet so good. The best tomato-based sauce should have that same perfect balance between sweetness and acidity, the same richness and lip-smacking savouriness of Heinz's famous tomato soup that I loved as a child.

Here in Sardinia, tomato sauce is made regularly and in bulk, and kept in the freezer, so that when there is nothing else in the house, or a friend brings you some ravioli

as a gift, you always have something at hand to dress it. It is so ubiquitous it is known simply as *sugo*, and I have met many Sardinians who eat this simple sugo with pasta every single day. Pasta al sugo remains many an Italian's favourite dish.

Though it takes care and attention to achieve the balance that makes tomato sauce so good, there is by no means any definitive method or recipe. There are infinite variations. Every cook in Italy has their own version. I make mine a different way almost every time I make it, which is at least once a week, and I adjust it depending on what I have to hand and what sort of mood I'm in. It is infinitely adaptable, and as long as you follow these essential building blocks, you cannot fail:

continued overleaf →

FAT

Fat is flavour. It is essential and is what gives your sauce depth. Fat brings out the best in the tomatoes, balances their acidity and provides richness. It could be in any form: whether butter, olive oil or the fat from sautéed pancetta. Some recipes add the fat at the end, such as swirling in a spoonful of mascarpone or double (heavy) cream just before serving.

AROMATICS

There are many herbs that work well with tomatoes and you can vary them according to preference and availability. My favourite hard herbs to use are rosemary, bay and sage. The soft herb basil is a classic, and mint is also good, especially when the sauce is paired with offal (such as *trippa alla romana*).

VEGETABLES

These help to provide a background flavour to your sauce. Just as you add carrots and celery to a stock to enhance the flavour of the meat, so you add vegetables to your sauce to enhance the flavour of your tomatoes. Carrot and onion are the most commonly used, and are often put in raw and then fished out later. If your tomatoes are not sweet to begin with, the onion and carrots will also add sweetness.

TOMATOES

The quality of the tomatoes is important. They should be whole, Italian, plum, peeled tomatoes. The 'juice' many of the cheaper varieties sit in is often made from unripe tomatoes and is sour and strong, affecting your finished sauce.

SWEETNESS

Good tomatoes will ensure you have the necessary sweetness to your sauce. Long and slow cooking will also coax out the sugars. If you do not have access to good tomatoes or you are short on time, sugar can be added. I frequently add a teaspoon of runny honey.

SAVOURINESS

Good tomato sauce needs good seasoning. Plenty of salt, or a savouriness that can be added with pancetta or anchovies. Adding grated Parmesan or pecorino when serving also emphasises this.

GARLIC

It is a mistake many make to add lots of garlic to tomato sauces. I love garlic, but have been very surprised by how little is actually used in Italian cooking. It is used very carefully, and in fairly sparing quantities, especially in tomato sauce. Most frequently a single clove is bashed and thrown in to the sautéing oil, then fished out before serving.

TEXTURE

A good sauce should be neither too thin or too thick. It can be chunky or smooth depending on your preference (pages 134–135) but never runny or watery. Simmering it slowly will help to lower the water content and to reduce your sauce to a good thickness.

For any of the following sauces on pages 134-135 you can, if you wish, pass the tomatoes through a mouli or vegetable mill to make them into a smooth and even paste. Many Italian cooks do this. I mostly keep mine whole because I like the chunks and hate the washing up, but I make an exception when I make Nonna's version, out of respect to her.

TOMATO SAUCE THREE WAYS

FRANCA'S TOMATO SAUCE

I make the following sauce in winter, which is aromatic with herbs and rich with pancetta and Parmesan. It's a sort of *amatriciana,* though it's what Franca uses as her everyday sauce.

SERVES 4–6

1 small onion, sliced
4 tablespoons olive oil
40 g (1½ oz) pancetta or guanciale, diced
2 bay leaves
1 small sprig rosemary
4–5 sage leaves
1 small dried chilli
800 g (1 lb 12 oz) tinned peeled tomatoes (pelati)
2 tablespoons water
1 Parmesan rind
sea salt

In a saucepan over a medium heat, fry the onion in the olive oil for a minute or two, then add the pancetta to the pan with the herbs and chilli and cook until the onion is soft and just beginning to turn golden, as is the fat on the pancetta or guanciale; this should take about 10–15 minutes. Add the tomatoes, using the water to rinse the tin or jar and pour it into the pan with the Parmesan rind. Leave to bubble away on a low heat for at least 30 minutes. Add salt to taste and remove the Parmesan rind, bay and rosemary. I like to eat the sage leaves so I leave them in.

MARCELLA'S TOMATO SAUCE (WITH SOME HELP FROM FRANCA)

Marcella Hazan is one of the queens of Italian cookery, and her rich, fresh and pure sauce, which uses simply butter, an onion and (preferably) fresh tomatoes, has rightly earned its place in the recipe hall of fame.

I had planned to include her recipe unaltered, as I'd made it long before living in Italy and loved it. However, the best laid plans often go awry.

When I tried to test the recipe at home, Franca was adamant I use olive oil. Marcella's inclusion of butter is no doubt a nod to her more Northern Italian roots (she was born in Emilia-Romagna). The further south one goes in Italy, the less butter one finds in cooking. As Franca says, when the olive oil is 'cosi buono', it doesn't seem to make sense. However, life is about compromises, and many of the best recipes are a meeting of minds. I have kept some of Marcella's butter, because I love the silky sweetness it gives, but added half olive oil too, to impart a bit of punch, pepper and depth. Hopefully, this way, everyone is happy.

SERVES 6

900 g (2 lb) chopped, ripe fresh tomatoes
    or 500 g (1 lb 1½ oz) tinned peeled tomatoes
40 g (1½ oz) butter
4 tablespoons best-quality olive oil
1 onion, halved
sea salt
Parmesan, grated, to serve

If using fresh tomatoes, wash them and cut them in half. Simmer them on a low heat in a covered saucepan for 10 minutes, until they are soft and collapsing.

Now puree the tomatoes through a mouli back into the pan. Add the butter, oil and the onion halves and cook at a very low heat, for around 45 minutes. If using tinned tomatoes simply pass them through a mouli beforehand and add all the ingredients into the pot at once.

Taste and season with salt. Discard the onion and serve with pasta of your choice, with plenty of grated Parmesan on top.

LUCA'S 'POVERI MA BELLI' TOMATO SAUCE

Based on Nonna's recipe, this is *sugo di pomodoro alla Sarda* (Sardinian style).

There's no great mystery to it: it is simply a case of using the best tinned tomatoes, the Sardinian Antonella brand naturally, and passing them through the mouli or vegetable mill to remove any of the bitter seeds. They are then cooked with some onion and finished with *olio buono* and salt. That's it.

Luca (like many Sardinians) maintains this is the best sauce in the world. It is also the best sauce for simple tomato pasta or for serving with Sardinian-style ravioli (including Culurgionis, page 128). It is pure and delicious. It's so simple that it doesn't detract from the ravioli filling either, which is very important for Sardinians. They hate flavours interfering with each other, or masking each other. You can add a leaf or two of basil when you serve it, along with the obligatory grated cheese.

SERVES 4–6

2 tablespoons olive oil, for frying
1 small white onion, peeled and halved
800 g (1 lb 12 oz) Antonella Tomatoes,
    passed through a mouli
3 tablespoons best-quality olive oil
sea salt

Heat the first batch of oil gently and place in the onion halves. Stir them around for a few minutes until they start to sizzle, then add the tomatoes. Cook at a very low simmer for half an hour or more, until the onion is completely tender and has collapsed into silky petals. Either remove the onion or blitz it into the sauce with a hand blender. I opt for the latter as I hate to throw it away.

Stir the sauce and add the very good olive oil and a good pinch of salt. Stir again and taste for seasoning. Add more salt if necessary.

Use as required.

LINGUINE WITH LEMON, BASIL, PECORINO AND MASCARPONE

Linguine con Limone, Pecorino e Basilico

To me, this will always be a dish known as the creamy-sweet taste of victory. There is, of course, a story behind it.

The recipe is a shameless plagiarism of Nigella's infamous Lemony Linguine.

Nigella is the only woman (apart from his beloved Mama, and his almost equally beloved former head chef, Florence Knight) whose recipes have won over Luca's fastidious Sardinian heart, and that's quite a feat. One night I decided to make her Lemony Linguine for supper. When he saw me adding cream, raw eggs and lemon juice to a bowl for the sauce he scoffed, shuffled to the table and began slicing himself some *salsiccia* (his fall-back meal and a form of protest if he disapproves of what I am cooking).

As I lifted the linguine out and tossed it vigorously in the creamy sauce, the scent of lemon and basil filling the air, I saw him watching me out of the corner of his eye, and slowly, silently, he set aside his sausage and sat, facing his empty plate expectantly. If prompting a Sardinian to surrender his salami isn't success, then I don't know what is.

I added mascarpone, because we had some that needed using, and basil because Luca suggested it and it went very well. You can of course just use cream, and leave out the basil.

SERVES 2, GENEROUSLY

2 egg yolks
100 ml (3½ fl oz/generous
  ½ cup) double (heavy) cream
2 tablespoons mascarpone
2 tablespoons grated pecorino
zest of 1 lemon, juice of ½
40 g (1½ oz) butter, cubed
250 g (8¾ oz) linguine
4 basil leaves, torn
sea salt, to taste

Bring a large pan of well-salted water to the boil.

Meanwhile, mix the yolks, cream, mascarpone, pecorino and lemon in a mixing bowl, whisking well to remove any lumps. Add the butter and place the bowl over your pan of boiling pasta, to gently warm the sauce, or in a nearby warm place.

When perfectly *al dente*, drain the pasta, reserving a little of the cooking water just in case (though I rarely need it here).

Throw the sauce into the pan with the drained pasta and stir vigorously, tossing the linguine well until every strand is coated and saucy. If things look too runny, put the pan over a very low heat and continue stirring and cooking for a moment or two longer. Add the torn basil leaves, check the seasoning, stir quickly and serve, smugly.

TROFIE WITH PESTO, TUNA AND TOMATOES

Trofie alla Carlofortina

One of the most beautiful towns in Sardinia is Carloforte, on the island of San Pietro.

Carloforte is famous for a handful of reasons. Firstly, for its history of tuna fishing, and secondly for coral, which was once abundant and collected and made into jewellery. Last but not least, for its cuisine.

In 1541 a handful of coral-fishing families left Liguria in search of coral and settled in Tabarka, off the coast of Tunisia. After exhausting the coral resources there, they began to hunt elsewhere, and discovered that there was an abundance of coral in the southern Sardinian sea. In 1739, they asked the then-king of Sardinia-Piedmonte, Charles Emmanuel III, to settle and build a commune on the island of San Pietro, and named their town in his honour: Charles the Strong (Carlo forte).

A variety of the Ligurian language is still spoken here, which is different to both Italian and Sardinian. The fishing families also brought with them their cuisine, most famously, their celebrated pesto.

The eponymous *Pasta alla Carlofortina* is a dish that celebrates both the history and bounty of the island. For the sauce, Genoese pesto is mixed with sweet local tomatoes and the infamous tuna, which is fished from the water surrounding San Pietro island. The pasta is usually homemade, often trofie, which is a Ligurian speciality. It's a really special dish, the marriage of tuna and cheese (the pesto contains both pecorino and Parmesan) may sound strange to some, but anyone who's ever enjoyed a tuna melt will know that this is a heavenly match. Tuna is such a meaty fish that it stands up brilliantly to the punchy flavours of basil, garlic and cheese. The tomatoes add a welcome sweetness, acidity and freshness.

Of course, you can easily buy trofie, or use any other type of pasta, but it's more fun to make your own. It's a very easy dough to make, but the shaping requires practice: the shape doesn't affect the flavour so don't be discouraged – even ugly trofie taste good. In terms of the technique for shaping them perfectly, I can only recommend watching a few Youtube videos before you start, and as is ever thus, practice eventually makes perfect.

FEEDS 4 MODESTLY HUNGRY PEOPLE, 2 OR 3 GREEDY ONES

For the trofie

300 g (10½ oz/2 cups) semola
di gran duro (semolina), plus
extra for dusting

For the sauce

100 g (3½ oz/⅔ cup) pine nuts
1 garlic clove
30 g (1 oz) pecorino, grated
30 g (1 oz) Parmesan, grated
2 large handfuls fresh
basil leaves, plus extra to
serve
70 ml (2½ fl oz/generous
¼ cup) extra virgin olive oil,
plus extra for frying
sea salt
1 handful of small, sweet
tomatoes, sliced
150 g (5¼ oz) best-quality
tinned tuna, halved

First, make your pasta. Mix the semolina and 145 g (5 oz/⅔ cup)
warm water in a bowl until it comes together to form a rough
dough. Take it out of the bowl and knead it on your worktop for
10 minutes or so, until you have an even, smooth dough. Wrap
it in cling film (plastic wrap) and set it aside for half an hour
while you make your pesto.

Blitz the nuts, garlic and cheese in a blender or mini food
processor until they form a rough breadcrumb consistency. Add
the basil and blitz for a second or two more, then add the oil and
salt and continue to mix until everything is incorporated. Do not
blitz for too long as you do not want a completely smooth paste –
a little texture is a good thing.

Now shape your trofie. Break off small pieces of the dough,
about the size of a hazelnut, and roll them into little twisted shapes.
Set them aside on a clean, semolina-dusted baking (cookie) sheet.

In a frying pan (skillet), soften your sliced tomatoes in a little
olive oil and a pinch of salt. Stir through the pesto and half of the
tuna, taste for seasoning, and set aside ready for your pasta.

Bring a large pan of salted water to the boil. Drop in your
trofie and cook for a minute or two until they bob to the surface
(if using bought pasta, follow the cooking instructions on the
packet). Fish them out using a slotted spoon and place them
straight into the pan with the sauce. Place this pan over the heat,
add a small ladle of the pasta cooking water and toss your pasta
and sauce by holding the pan and flicking your wrist, until
it is well combined and beautifully saucy. Serve with the rest
of the tuna and a scattering of basil leaves.

NOTE
When cooking this for the first time, my
mum asked if she could eat the sage leaves,
and the answer is yes. They are
in fact my favourite bit.

140

PASTA WITH BUTTER TO SAVE AND SALVE

Pasta al Burro e Salvia

I love butter. I come from a family of butter-fiends. My mother eats it in chunks from the pat, with a spoon, and my father spreads it as thick as cheese on his toast.

Italian butter is very different to the kind readily available in England. Maybe (probably) I'm just getting old, but I'm sure lots of butter in England doesn't taste of anything anymore. In my last months before moving to Sardinia, I got into a habit of smelling the butter in shops. I would unfold some of the paper and have a good sniff of the pat inside. It drew some strange looks from other shoppers, but it's a sound method of judging the quality. A good butter has an unmistakable smell. It should smell of thick, cold, cream: ever-so-slightly cheesy, faintly sweet. I urge you to start smelling your butters. The butter out here smells very strongly, as butter should. It is purest white, always unsalted, and comes in enormous 500 g (1 lb 1¾ oz) blocks, wrapped in white waxed paper, like the butter of old. It is a beautiful thing to look at, and to eat.

Butter only appeared in culinary use in Italy in the Renaissance, and was initially used by the wealthy, often made into an elaborate table centrepiece rather than being consumed – yes, butter sculptures! To this day, despite its quality and ready availability, the Sardinians very rarely use butter in cooking. When butter is used, it is as an essential flavour in the finished dish, rather than just a means of cooking.

Glamorous it may not be, but I could happily eat this dish every day for the rest of my life. It also demonstrates perfectly the essential (and often overlooked) skill in making pasta sauces, and the first thing everyone learns when they start cooking pasta in Italy; that the pasta cooking water must be added to the finished dish, to both emulsify the sauce and melt the grated cheese into a creamy consistency. Once you have learnt how to do this, you will never look back.

The earthiness of the sage is what really grounds this recipe, so don't be tempted to leave it out. The echo of a 'salve', seems fitting too, as this dish is deepest comfort.

FOR 2 RESTRAINED DINERS, OR 1 HUNGOVER/FRAGILE ONE

220 g (7¾ oz) dried pasta of your choice (I like risoni or any 'short' pasta best)
120 g (4¼ oz) butter
8–10 small sage leaves
70 g (2½ oz) Parmesan, grated, plus extra to serve
sea salt

Bring a large saucepan of well-salted water to the boil. Drop in the pasta.

Place the butter in a wide, shallow pan and put on the lowest heat. Add the sage and cook for a moment or so to gently to release the aromas. Drain the pasta when it is at your perfect *al dente*, reserving a cup of the cooking liquid. Add half the cooking water and the pasta to the pan with the butter and sage and turn up the heat. Stir and toss well for a minute or so, then add the cheese and toss again and again, until an emulsified and silky sauce forms. If it looks too dry, add more of the cooking water, too wet, carry on cooking. Serve with more cheese.

RED WINE AND RADICCHIO RISOTTO WITH SAPA

Risotto al Vino Rosso, Sapa e Radicchio

I love red wine: drinking it, cooking it, even painting with it. Sardinian Cannonau is one of the most drinkable red wines I know. It's smooth, rich and rounded and…. just very easy to drink, whether on its own or with food. I've honestly never tasted a bad one – even those that arrive in opaque unlabelled petrol containers are delicious. Like the Greeks, Sards often drink this wine chilled, especially in the summer. Gianni cuts up ripe peaches and puts them into his glass, which makes a delicious sort-of pudding.

This wine is also wonderful in cooking. In this risotto, the fruitiness of red wine and the richness of butter and cheese balances the bitterness of beautiful purple radicchio.

I cook the radicchio separately, in a little butter and sapa, just to take the edge off and to enhance its own fruitiness.

SERVES 4 AS A MAIN, 6 AS A PRIMO

1.2 litres (40½ fl oz/5 cups) light chicken stock
500 ml (17 fl oz/2 cups) red wine (preferably Cannonau)
150 g (5¼ oz) butter
½ head of large radicchio or 1 small entire head, finely sliced
pinch of sea salt
1 tablespoon sapa or an aged balsamic
2 small white onions, finely diced
2 garlic cloves, sliced
400 g (14 oz/2 cups) risotto rice
80 g (3 oz) Parmesan, grated, plus extra to serve

In a deep saucepan over a low heat, mix together your stock and wine.

Melt 20 g (¾ oz) butter in a separate saucepan. Reserve a handful of radicchio for decoration then fry the rest until it just wilts. Add a pinch of salt and the sapa. Continue cooking for a minute or so and set aside.

Melt 50 g (1¾ oz) butter in a deep saucepan and fry the onions and garlic gently, until soft and translucent. Add the rice and stir for a minute or so. Add a ladle of your wine and stock mixture and stir until it has been absorbed into the rice. Repeat the process, ladle by ladle, stirring after each addition until the rice absorbs the liquid.

The whole cooking process should take around 17–20 minutes. Once your rice is al dente and the liquid has mostly evaporated, set it aside for the 'mantecatura', or 'creaming'.

With a wooden spoon, beat in the rest of the butter and grated Parmesan. Beat well, for a minute or two, until a luscious creamy sauce is formed.

Finally, fold in your cooked radicchio and serve, topped with the reserved raw radicchio for decoration and an extra grating of Parmesan.

FREGOLA WITH CLAMS AND FENNEL

Fregola con Arselle e Finocchio

Apart from its wonderful flavours, there's something very pleasing about the shapes and textures of this dish, with its pebbles of fregola and sweet, soft clam nuggets. The fennel provides a heady anise back-note. Here, the fregola is cooked like a risotto, the grains added with the base ingredients and cooked out gently with liquid until they become plump and just *al dente*. It is a deliciously soupy, salty, sweet combination. If you like, you can add some grated bottarga on top.

SERVES 6 AS A STARTER, OR 4 AS A MAIN

For the clams

3 tablespoons extra virgin
  olive oil
1 garlic clove
1.5 kg (3 lb 5 oz) clams, cleaned
  and broken shells removed
200 ml (6¾ fl oz/¾ cup)
  dry white wine
  (preferably Vementino)

For the fregola

1 garlic clove, finely sliced
2 large fennel bulbs, finely
  diced and green leafy
  stalks reserved
50 g (1¾ oz) butter
2 tablespoons olive oil,
  plus extra to serve
350 g (12½ oz) fregola
1 litre (34 fl oz/4 cups) fish
  or vegetable stock, or water
small bunch flat leaf parsley,
  chopped
zest and juice of ½ lemon,
  to serve
sea salt (optional) and freshly
  ground pepper

Heat the oil in a wide, lidded frying pan (skillet) over a medium heat. Add the garlic and cook for 30 seconds, until fragrant. Throw in the clams, add the wine, cover the pan and turn up the heat. After a minute or so at high heat, take off the lid to check if the clams are done – they should be open. If they are still closed, put the lid on again and cook for a little longer. Once they are all cooked remove from the heat and strain the juice into a container. Add this juice to your fregola cooking liquid (whether using stock or water). Drizzle the clams with some good oil to keep them juicy and put to one side with the lid on for the moment.

In a deep saucepan over a medium heat, fry the garlic and fennel in the butter and oil. Cook until the fennel is translucent and just beginning to take colour, around 5 minutes.

Add the fregola and stir well. Now add your cooking liquid, ladle by ladle, and continue cooking over a medium heat, stirring all the time, as though you were making risotto.

When the fregola is just al dente and the mixture is nice and soupy, which should take around 12–15 minutes, stir through your clams with a little chopped parsley and lemon zest. Add a squeeze of lemon juice and taste for seasoning (I rarely add extra salt as the clams are salty).

Serve in bowls with some of the reserved fennel fronds scattered over the top, and an extra drizzle of good olive oil.

SAFFRON, ORANGE AND MASCARPONE RISOTTO

Risotto allo Zafferano

I don't make or eat risotto often, a plate of pasta being – to my mind at least – much easier to produce. The constant stirring it requires demands more attention and patience than I am usually willing to allow. When I do make or eat it, I want it to be perfect; creamy, rich and unctuous (this is quite possibly the only time the word 'unctuous' is acceptable).

This dish is a brilliant sunshine yellow, and has all the flavour and golden glory of the very best examples of risotto. The (other) most tiresome thing about risotto is that it necessitates good stock, but once you have this under your belt, the rest is really very easy.

SERVES 6 AS A PRIMO, 4 AS A MAIN

1.5 litres (50¾ fl oz/6½ cups) light chicken stock
110 g (4 oz) butter
2 small white onions, finely diced
400 g (14 oz/2 cups) risotto rice
scant ½ teaspoon saffron powder, or a good pinch of saffron strands dissolved in hot water
150 ml (5 fl oz/⅔ cup) vermouth, or white wine
1 heaped tablespoon mascarpone
80 g (3 oz) Parmesan, grated
zest and juice of 1 small, sweet orange
1 teaspoon sea salt

Pour the stock into a deep saucepan over a medium heat.

Melt 70 g (2½ oz) butter in another deep saucepan and fry the onions gently, until soft and translucent. Add the rice and saffron and stir for a minute or so. Add the wine and cook until it has been absorbed into the rice, stirring all the time. Add the now hot stock, ladle by ladle, stirring after each addition until the rice absorbs the liquid.

The whole cooking process should take around 17–20 minutes. Once your rice is *al dente* and the liquid has mostly evaporated, set it aside for the '*mantecatura*', or 'creaming'.

With a wooden spoon, beat in the rest of the butter, mascarpone and Parmesan. Beat well, for a minute or two, until a luscious creamy sauce is formed. Add some of the orange juice and half the zest, check the seasoning, adding salt and more orange juice to taste, and serve with an extra dollop of mascarpone and the rest of the zest scattered over the top.

PERFECT
POLENTA

Polenta Perfetta

Polenta is a wonderful, misunderstood ingredient. Often dismissed as bland or lumpy, it needs a little love and a generous hand to be coaxed into deliciousness.

There are two main ways of preparing polenta:

1. Cooking it with liquid and then setting it hard, to be cut up and grilled, fried or baked.
2. Cooking it with plenty of liquid and serving it hot and runny, the consistency of wet porridge.

The latter is better, for me at least. Like so many other basic carbohydrates that have formed the pillars of a peasant diet for thousands of years, polenta was designed essentially as a filler (much like pasta) but, like pasta, it can be so much more. It needs the lift of lemon zest, the creamy richness of butter or olive oil (or both) and preferably some form of cheese for it to be understood for the delicious foodstuff it really is. Follow this recipe and you will become a polenta addict, as I am.

Polenta is available in numerous forms, the most common being white polenta, quick-cook or instant polenta and slow-cook/coarser polenta. The latter is lovely, though takes much longer to prepare. The instant stuff has less flavour, but is still good for everyday cooking. The following recipe works for any type, just check the cooking instructions on the back of the pack for timings.

If you are cooking this to serve with fish, do not add the Parmesan, but instead add the zest of half a lemon, and a little extra olive oil instead.

SERVES 8 AS A STARTER, 6 AS A MAIN

300 g (10½ oz/2½ cups)
  polenta
2 scant teaspoons sea salt
150 g (5¼ oz) butter
100 g (3½ oz) Parmesan,
  grated
extra virgin olive oil,
  for drizzling

Bring 2 litres (68 fl oz/8 cups) water to the boil in a large deep saucepan. Pour in the polenta in a steady stream, whisking all the time. Turn the heat down to low, and cook for 20–40 minutes (depending on the polenta you use), whisking occasionally, until it has become a lovely, smooth, wet porridge consistency. Add the salt, butter, Parmesan and a good drizzle of oil. Stir well to combine. Taste for seasoning, keep warm and serve in deep bowls, accompanied by the braise/stew of your choice.

POLENTA, SAUSAGE, CHEESE AND TOMATO BAKE

Polenta alla Campidanese

A dish for polenta lovers, for cheese lovers, and for lovers of sausage.

A dish for everyone, then.

The sauce is much like the other *Campidanese* recipe (page 122) that is served with malloreddus; a rich sausage ragù that cloaks the polenta and mingles into the melting cheese.

Franca always makes her polenta for this dish with homemade lard from the family pigs. If you prefer, you can make it with butter or olive oil. The important thing is that it is rich and tasty.

This can be made well in advance (like lasagne) and stored in the fridge or freezer.

SERVES 8

For the polenta

350 g (12½ oz) polenta
4 tablespoons grated
   Parmesan
100 g (3½ oz) butter or lard
sea salt

For the ragù

1 small onion, diced
1 carrot, diced
1 garlic clove, finely chopped
1 celery stick, diced
4 tablespoons olive oil
2 bay leaves
1 small dried red chilli
1 sprig of sage
400 g (14 oz) sausage meat
100 ml (3½ fl oz/⅓ cup) white
   wine
1 kg (2 lb 3¼ oz) tinned
   tomatoes
sea salt
pinch of caster (superfine)
   sugar (optional)

To serve

300 g (10½ oz) mozzarella,
   cut into rough chunks
handful of basil leaves
100 g (3½ oz) pecorino, grated

Preheat the oven to 190°C (375°F/Gas 5).

First, make the polenta. Place 1.8 litres (61 fl oz/7½ cups) water in a deep saucepan and bring to the boil. Pour in the polenta in a steady stream, whisking all the time. Turn the heat down to low and continue whisking every few minutes until the polenta is cooked. This varies depending on the type and brand of polenta, but there should be cooking times on the package. It's normally between 10–30 minutes.

While the polenta is cooking, start your ragù. In a large frying pan (skillet), cook the onion, carrot, garlic and celery in the olive oil with the bay leaf, chilli and sage until the vegetables are soft and translucent, around 10 minutes.

Add the sausagemeat and cook for another 10 minutes or so, until just beginning to turn golden. Add the wine and cook for a minute or two. Now add the tomatoes with 3–4 tablespoons water and leave to simmer for 40–50 minutes. Taste and adjust the seasoning accordingly – depending on your tomatoes, you may need to add a touch of sugar here – then take off the heat.

When the polenta is cooked, add the Parmesan, lard or butter and a large pinch of salt. Stir well. Pour the polenta out into a greased, deep roasting tin and set aside to cool and set solid, around 20 minutes. Once solid, tip it out onto a chopping board and slice it into batons about the size of a slender custard slice, about 4 cm (1½ in).

Lay half of the slices 2½ cm (1 in) apart in a large, deep gratin dish. Pour over half of your finished sauce and dot over half of the mozzarella, basil, and pecorino. Make another layer using the rest of the slices, the sauce and the rest of the cheeses. Sprinkle over the remaining fresh basil leaves and place in the preheated oven for 35–45 minutes, until golden and bubbling. Allow to cool for a minute or two before serving.

AT BEST IGNORED, AT WORST A NUISANCE

Foraging was an important part of my childhood. Like me, both my parents are also happy to spend hours of their free time with an empty ice-cream carton in hand, ferreting their way through bushes and hedgerows.

Foraging in Sardinia is common. The wild countryside and warm climate make it the perfect breeding ground for numerous edible weeds and funghi. In late autumn and early spring, you'll often see lines of cars parked along stretches of land that are known to be good for a particular mushroom or wild herb.

I often bump into fellow foragers, who tell me what they have found and where, and give me some of their haul. They advise me how to cook this mushroom (sliced, breadcrumbed and deep-fried) or how to differentiate between *ferula* (deadly) and wild fennel (delicious).

Asides from this camaraderie, foraging offers many rewards. There is the satisfaction felt from finding food for free. There is the activity itself, which involves walking and being outdoors (something I love). There is also the element of discovery, which never loses its charm.

The other driving force for me and I'm sure for most foragers – and the thing that is at the forefront of almost any activity I do – is greed.

Even Luca, who is the antithesis of 'outdoorsy' – a man who dislikes the beach because it is, 'full of sands', can be enticed to forage if there is the prospect of a plate of wild asparagus pasta at the end of it.

There is something incredibly satisfying about picking plants that are at best ignored, and at worst a nuisance, and making good use of them. Many people swear by the health properties of eating weeds.

In Italy, confusingly, the word *radice* is used to describe any plant with a succulent root and bitter leaves, such as all of the radicchio family and dandelions. There is a shepherd on the island whose sheep feed only on wild radice, and his

cheese is reported to be the best in Sardinia. *Erbe* refers to any delicately leafy, salad-type plant, including grass. Wild fennel, sorrel, borage, purslane and wild asparagus all grow in our part of Sardinia, and I have found most of them in England too.

CHICKPEAS WITH WILD FENNEL AND HAM

Ceci con Finocchio e Guanciale

It is a myth universally acknowledged that buying any old chickpeas (garbanzo beans), soaking them overnight and boiling them for an hour the next day will result in soft and yielding goodness.

There are chickpeas and *chickpeas* in this world, and the former are too often disappointing. The trick is to choose good dried ones in the first place. Beware of small, rock-hard, dark pellets. Look for uniform, pale creamy-brown and amply sized specimens. They should be nicely nubbly. I don't trust the smooth ones. Soak them in plenty of cold water for 24 hours, and then cook them according to the below instructions and you will never be disappointed by a sub-par chickpea again.

There is truly an art to cooking pulses, one which the Sardinians have mastered. I love cooking them as they are the perfect metaphor for what cookery is all about: layering. The pulses are the blank canvas on which you can apply layers of flavour depending on what you have to hand, and what there is growing at the time.

These are simply known as *ceci*, and are a very traditional Sardinian recipe for the last few weeks of winter and the very beginning of Spring. In Luca's family, a pig is always killed just after new year, and some of its salt-cured skin goes into the cooking of these chickpeas. I have substituted it here with guanciale, but if you have access to good pig skin, go right ahead. Just as peas and ham are a perfect combination so are chickpeas and ham. The nutty sweetness is then lifted by wild fennel, which grows in the grass verges.

Traditionally in Sardinia, pulses and beans were always cooked in terracotta pots, as it is said to impart a better flavour. Initially sceptical, I'm now a convert – they honestly do make things taste better. It's a nice thing to have a special clay pot just for cooking beans. I'm a great believer in having special pots for all sorts of things; it makes life in the kitchen more interesting.

You can adapt this according to what you have in the kitchen at the time – it is very flexible.

SERVES 6

1 onion, diced
4 garlic cloves, sliced
2 bay leaves
2 celery sticks, diced
1 small dried red chilli
large handful of chopped wild fennel, or 1 fennel bulb, chopped and added with its fronds, plus extra to serve
4 tablespoons olive oil, plus extra to serve
50 g (1¾ oz) guanciale or pancetta, diced (optional)
500 g (1 lb 1¾ oz) chickpeas (garbanzo beans), soaked in cold water for 24 hours and drained
2 bay leaves
3 sundried tomatoes
sea salt

In a deep frying pan (skillet) over a medium heat, cook the onion, garlic, bay leaves, celery, chilli and fennel in the olive oil until soft, around 10 minutes.

Add the guanciale or pancetta (if using) and continue to fry over a low heat until it is just beginning to colour, around 5 minutes.

Add the drained chickpeas, the sundried tomatoes, and 1 litre (34 fl oz/4 cups) water. Cook, partially covered, over a low heat for 1 hour or more, until the chickpeas are completely tender. Add salt to taste. Eat, with a drizzle of your best olive oil and some fresh fronds of fennel (and some cheese if you wish).

154

BROWN LENTIL, SAGE AND CHESTNUT SOUP WITH RICOTTA

Zuppa di Lenticchie, Salvia, Castagne e Ricotta

The best sort of nourishing brown sludge. If dishes could speak, this one would say 'welcome home'.

Follow it with the first clementines of the season and a square or two of *panforte*, and you have a perfect winter dinner.

You can either boil or roast your own chestnuts from raw, or do it the cheat's way and buy them ready cooked. Whilst I love eating the fresh roasted ones, I don't love peeling them to cook with, so I buy them pre-prepared for this recipe.

SERVES 4–6

250 g (8¾ oz) small
  brown lentils
1 onion, diced
1 carrot, scrubbed and diced
1 celery stick, diced
3 tablespoons olive oil,
  plus extra to serve
2 bay leaves
50 g (1¾ oz) pancetta,
  cubed or diced
120 ml (4¼ f l oz/½ cup)
  red wine
700 ml (24 fl oz/3 cups)
  chicken or vegetable stock,
  or water
150 g (5¼ oz) cooked,
  peeled chestnuts
sea salt
100 g (3½ oz) ricotta
fried sage leaves (optional)

Place the lentils in a bowl and fill with cold water. Discard any strange floaty bits or shrivelled specimens. Drain and set aside.

In a saucepan over a medium heat, fry the onion, carrot and celery in the olive oil with the sage. Stir to coat in the oil and add the diced pancetta. Cook for a good 10 minutes or so, until the pancetta just begins to colour. Add the bay leaves, lentils, wine and stock with 100 g (3½ oz) of the chestnuts, reserving the remainder for decoration and texture at the end. Bring to a simmer and cook for around 30–40 minutes, until the lentils are just soft.

Season the lentils well with salt and serve, with some blobs of ricotta, and extra drizzle of olive oil and the rest of the chestnuts, finely chopped, on top. You can also fry some extra sage leaves and use these for garnish too, if you like.

EGGS IN TOMATO SAUCE WITH MUSIC PAPER BREAD

Pane Frattau

All around the world, one finds different versions of a tomato-and-egg-based dish. There is the well-loved shakshuka and the Italian 'eggs in purgatory'. And then there is the Sardinian *pane frattau* (broken bread in Sardo). The story of this dish is a charming one. The shepherds carried their sheets of pane carasau in their saddle bags whilst away from home watching their herds. After eating the bigger pieces, the broken shards that remained in the bottom of the bags were soaked in broth, layered with tomato sauce and cheese and cooked with an egg on top. A dish born of necessity and economy.

Traditionally the tomato sauce is layered between leftover shards of pane carasau, which are softened in meat broth, then the whole lot is baked and subsequently topped with a poached egg and some grated pecorino before serving.

I have updated and tweaked the traditional method slightly to allow for those of us who don't always have broth on hand, and also to minimise effort, with everything cooked in the same dish. Thus, there is no need for poaching the egg.

An excellent brunch, or a good solo lunch. Almost like a cheat's lasagne, much quicker to make, vegetarian, and just as good.

You will be surprised how much liquid the pane carasau absorbs – it becomes almost pasta-like in texture.

Though it's not traditional, I like this with a good pinch of chilli flakes on top.

SERVES 4

---

1 x quantity Nonna's tomato sauce (page 135)
800 ml (27 fl oz/3⅓ cups) hot stock, ideally homemade, but fine with good quality shop-bought
8 sheets of pane carasau
150 g (5¼ oz) pecorino, grated
handful of basil leaves, torn
sea salt
4 eggs
pinch of chilli flakes (optional)
green salad, to serve

Preheat the oven to 200°C (400°F/Gas 6).

Warm up your sauce and your stock in separate saucepans.

Choose a nice deep gratin dish (I always make this in a round terracotta one). Cover the bottom with a layer of pane carasau. Spoon over a generous ladle of the warm stock and let it soak in. Then spoon over a ladleful of your tomato sauce and sprinkle over a handful of the cheese. Add a shred or two of basil.

Repeat this process, layering up the bread soaked with stock, the sauce and cheese as though you were making lasagne. Save some cheese and basil for the very top.

I normally make around 4–6 layers. When you have finished layering, if there is any stock left, drizzle it around the sides and edges to make sure everything is nice and saucy.

Finally, make little dents in the top of the dish to contain your eggs. Crack the eggs into their little nooks, sprinkle over the remaining cheese and basil, add a pinch of salt on the yolks and a little pinch of chilli flakes, if using, and place in the preheated oven for 20–30 minutes, until the eggs whites are set. Eat with a green salad.

FIVE

TERRA

Meat is a large part of the Sardinian diet. Mutton, for some reason, is eaten little in England, though it was once very popular. In Sardinia there is still a great tradition of eating mutton, or simply *pecora*, as it is known. These adult pecora live a noble, free-range existence in the Sardinian hills before they hand in their dinner pails. The flavour is really special. Pork and lamb are the most common, with the occasional chicken and bit of beef, horse or donkey thrown in (Sards are not squeamish). The scale of meat farming is still relatively small, and many are lucky in that most of our meat comes from our own animals (reared free range and slaughtered on the farm).

Suckling pig is Sardinia's most iconic dish. Usually spit-roast over an open fire, it is the centrepiece of any Sardinian celebration. Luca, like many Italians, has a habit of calling everything 'small'. I think this must stem from the Italian penchant for diminutives. Even the word small (*piccola*) becomes 'little small' – *piccolina*. A naughty girl, *monella*, often becomes a naughty small girl: *monellina*. A beer, *birra*, often becomes

a *birretta*. Luca (like most Sardinian men) spends much of his life in *giro* (around and about) going for 'small beers' or 'small sandwiches' followed by 'small sleeps', and whenever we are invited to a dinner or lunch, it is inevitable that we will eat a 'small pig'. Describing these things as 'small' somehow makes them endearing (and escapes reproach – 'but *amore*, it was only a small beer') and in the case of the 'small pig', it is delicious too. The pigs are normally raised at home, then slaughtered once they reach the right size. Alberto (Luca's brother) has a few litters a year and feeds them on food scraps and home-grown rice. Then he will slaughter about two thirds of them and raise the rest to be adults. After being cleaned and well salted, the pigs are slow roasted over the open fire, and once the skin is as brittle as glass, they are served, normally on a large cork platter lined with branches of myrtle. The myrtle perfumes the meat, which is deliciously tender and moist. It is an experience that cannot be missed.

It goes without saying, but try to seek out good-quality, ethically reared meat. It will taste better, too.

BAKED CHICKEN WITH CITRUS, FENNEL AND WHITE WINE

Pollo con Arancia Amara, Finocchio, Vino Bianco e Olive

Sardinians love to braise meat with olives, to impart a delicious, olive-scented saltiness, and they also love to cook fennel beneath braising meat, so it becomes soft and sweet from the meat juices. This chicken tray-bake with orange and fennel – which is based on a brilliant Nigella recipe, a favourite when I lived in England – gets the Sardinian treatment, and it's now become a staple in our home.

SERVES 4–6

zest and juice of 1 lemon, and 1 normal orange, or 1 Seville orange
3 teaspoons Dijon mustard
4 tablespoons extra virgin olive oil, plus extra for drizzling
2 teaspoons sea salt
2 teaspoons fennel seeds
650 ml (22 fl oz/2¾ cups) white wine
2 fennel bulbs, fronds reserved to serve
8 bone-in, skin-on chicken thighs
handful of green olives

Make a marinade with the citrus juice and zest, mustard, oil, salt, fennel seeds and wine.

Slice each fennel bulb into quarters lengthways, and then each quarter lengthways into three.

Place the chicken, the fennel slices and the marinade in a sealable plastic bag, and chill in the fridge for a couple of hours, preferably overnight.

The next day, preheat the oven to 200°C (400°F/Gas 6).

Decant the entire contents of the bag into a roasting tin, arranging the chicken skin-side up, on top. Scatter over the olives, willy-nilly. Drizzle an extra bit of oil on top of the chicken (to help it brown). Place the dish in the oven and cook for 1 hour, until the chicken is brown and the fennel is tender.

Remove from the oven and reduce the sauce for a minute or two, either by placing the whole dish over the hob, or decanting the liquid and reducing it into a separate saucepan. It should become a delicious sticky 'gravy' consistency.

Serve, with the sauce drizzled over, and some fresh fennel fronds on top.

ROAST CHICKEN
AND OTHER STORIES...

I was raised on Sunday roasts, and 'a roast' is still my dad's favourite meal.

When I moved here, I realised that the Sardinians do not do roasts in the same way. Yes, there is roasted meat, and occasionally roasted potatoes, but both are roasted in olive oil and have a very different flavour. Most significantly, there is no gravy. Ever. Gravy does not exist in Italian culture. For my dad, this is a crushing blow; he is a man with a passion for gravy. When I first took Luca to meet him, he cooked us roast lamb. To Luca it was a revelation:

'What was this 'sauce'? he asked, incredulously.

'It's not sauce, you fool, it's GRRRAAAAAVY!' my father bellowed proudly in reply.

Luca still talks reverently about what he thereafter affectionately named, 'THE gravy sauce'.

One day I decided that I wanted to cook a sort of 'Britalian' dinner for my Sardinian family.

Roast chicken, with an Italian twist, and a sort of hybrid gravy-sauce. I begged some fresh rosemary from our neighbour, who appeared with her arms full and asked me what I intended to do with it. I explained that I had a very good way of roasting chicken with anchovy, rosemary, lemon and butter. She nodded appreciatively as I listed the first three ingredients then recoiled in horror as I mentioned the 'b' word. 'Nooooo, noooo very bad! Butter very bad - olive oil! Only and always!' she wagged her finger at me. I remained determined.

Next, I had to find the chicken. I rooted around in our freezer and found a nice-looking number that I thought would do perfectly. I left it out to defrost overnight and went to bed.

At about midnight, Luca came home from work and discovered the chicken thawing innocently on the kitchen side.

'Letiiiizia', he growled, as he came into the bedroom, 'why you take my father's chicken out of the freezer and leave LIKE THIS?!'

'Well', I muttered sleepily,
'I thought I would cook it for
us tomorrow night'.

'For us?! This my father's chicken,
he grow himself, and my brother
kill with his hands, and you want
to eat it for us only? This chicken
feed NINE PEOPLE! And tomorrow is
TUESDAY! You cannot do this! This
is not England, ehhh'.

At lunchtime the next day, we
were at Nonna's discussing where
and how to cook the sacred chicken,
and who to invite to eat it. Family
members were summoned. Two visiting
Italian friends happened to be
arriving that night. As is the way
in Sardinia, a party easily assembled.
Fifteen people drifted in, bringing
bread, wine, cheese, salami. I set
to work with my chicken. Everything
was intact; neck on, guts still
inside, feet attached. Much of the
meat I'd dealt with before was
vac-packed, sanitised, totally
disconnected to the animal it came
from. This chicken was definitely
an animal, and I felt strange dealing
with it. I began to understand Luca's
insistence that such a thing should
be cooked, and eaten, with respect.

I realised it was a significant
moment. To my Sardinian family, this
chicken represented much more than
just a chicken. It represented hard
work, celebration, gratitude and
family. I began thinking maybe this
was probably what all food should
represent. Across the table,
Nonna beamed at me, toothlessly.

We all ate some chicken. The anchovy,
lemon and rosemary butter complimented
it perfectly, and mingled with the
chicken juices to create the most
delicious 'gravy-sauce'. Everybody
loved it, and this culinary blending
of my two beloved countries remains
one of my favourite recipes, as
well as a valuable lesson in taking
nothing for granted.

A KIND OF ITALIAN ROAST CHICKEN

Pollo Arrosto con Burro al Rosmarino e Acciughe

The perfect thing for a relaxed gathering. Plenty of wine, fresh bread and a green or bitter salad are the only other things necessary.

SERVES 6–8

1 chicken, roughly 1.6 kg
  (3 lb 8 oz)
sea salt and freshly ground
  black pepper

*For the rosemary, anchovy,
garlic and lemon butter*

1 small tin anchovies
  (or 12–14 fillets)
1 small lemon, zest and juice
2 garlic cloves
200 g (7 oz) butter
2 tablespoons
  chopped rosemary

Preheat the oven to 180°C (350°F/Gas 4).

Season the chicken lightly all over, inside and out.

Put all the butter ingredients into a blender and blitz until smooth. Taste for seasoning.

Stuff some of the butter inside the cavity, under the skin and all over the breast. Smear the rest all over the chicken with your hands.

Place the bird breast-side down in a roasting tin and cook for 45 minutes. Remove from the oven, baste the bird all over with the juices, and then turn it breast-side up. Turn up the oven to 200°C (400°F/Gas 6) and roast for another 20 minutes. Insert a skewer into the fattest part of the thigh and press; if the juices run clear, the bird is done. If not, then put back in the oven for a little longer. Once cooked, leave to rest for a few minutes before carving and serving with all of its delicious juices.

POACHED CHICKEN WITH FREGOLA, MINT AND AIOLI

Fregola in Brodo, Pollo Lesso e Aioli

Poaching is a wonderful and often forgotten way of cooking meat. It is incredibly simple, surprisingly quick, and ensures meat is always juicy and flavoursome. It also means you have, in a matter of moments, created either more than one meal, or at least two courses, simultaneously. This is because poaching also gives you delicious stock, or cooking liquor, with which you can make minestra or soup, or simply serve as broth. Here, the cooking liquid is used to cook fregola to be eaten as a first course, and the deliciously tender meat is served as a secondo.

Chickens are kept by many households in Sardinia and killed for special occasions. If your attendance incites a friend or family member to kill a chicken, you should feel greatly honoured.

Traditionally, after being poached, the cooked chicken would be wrapped in myrtle leaves to perfume the meat. If you grow myrtle, I highly recommend trying it. The aioli, while perhaps not traditional, is a delicious accompaniment.

SERVES 4

1 chicken, roughly 1.6 kg
  (3 lb 8 oz)
1 onion, peeled and halved
1 carrot, scraped and halved
1 potato, washed and peeled
2 sticks of celery heart, halved
sea salt
handful of parsley stalks
150 g (5¼ oz) fregola
handful of mint leaves
extra virgin olive oil, to drizzle

For the aioli

2 egg yolks
1 scant teaspoon sea salt
1 teaspoon mustard (optional)
2 garlic cloves, minced
200 ml (7 fl oz/¾ cup) best-
  quality extra virgin olive oil
100 ml (3½ fl oz/scant ½ cup)
  neutral oil, such as sunflower
2 tablespoons lemon juice

Remove your chicken from the fridge and allow it to come to room temperature. Add the bird, the vegetables, a good pinch of salt and the parsley stalks to a large stock pot or saucepan (it must be big enough to accommodate everything) and fill with water. The chicken and veg must be completely submerged.

Bring to a rolling boil, put a lid on it and then turn the heat right down to the very lowest possible setting. Leave to cook for 1 hour.

After this time, check that your chicken is cooked by puncturing the fattest part of the thigh and seeing if the juices run clear.

If it is cooked, remove it, wrap it loosely in aluminium foil and set it aside. Continue to simmer the stock until you have a good, meaty, savoury flavour.

When you are happy with the flavour and depth of your stock (remember to be attentive with the salt), add the fregola.

Stir well and cook until the fregola is just al dente, stirring all the time (this should take about 7–10 minutes). Chop half of the mint leaves and stir into the fregola. Taste and check for seasoning, adding more salt if necessary.

Serve the fregola and broth in bowls, drizzled with some extra oil, as a *primi*.

To make the aioli, place the yolks in a small bowl or the jug of a blender. Add the salt, mustard (if using) and garlic and start whisking. Drizzle the oil in drop by drop until it is emulsified, blitzing or whisking vigorously all the while. Add the lemon juice. Mix and taste for seasoning. Add more lemon or salt according to your preference. If you like, dilute with cold water to make it runnier.

Next, carve the chicken and arrange on a serving platter. Drizzle with your best olive oil, sprinkle with some sea salt flakes and scatter with the rest of the mint. Serve with the aioli.

QUAIL WITH CAPERS

Quaglia al Vino con Capperi

These tiny, perfect birds are both are cheap and tasty. They also encourage eating with the fingers and general bone-gnawing, which is my favourite way to eat.

    This is a classic Sardinian way of cooking them, where the capers and quail juices melt into a delicious, piquant sauce mellowed with garlic and booze. The best quail dish I have ever come across, and the simplest.

    Serve with a bitter leaf salad and bread for mopping up juices.

SERVES 2

2 quails
sea salt
3 tablespoons olive oil
2 garlic cloves, halved
handful of chopped parsley
1 tablespoon capers
2 small glasses of Vernaccia,
   or another dry white wine
   or sherry
bitter leaf salad, to serve
crusty bread, to serve

Season the quails all over with salt.

    Heat the oil in a deep frying pan (skillet) with a lid over a medium heat and add the garlic. Let it sizzle away for a minute, until fragrant.

    Add the quails to the pan and brown them in the garlic and oil, making sure to turn the garlic and birds routinely so they don't catch. When both are golden all over, add the chopped parsley, the capers and the wine. Place the lid half on the pan and leave to bubble away for 8 minutes or so.

    Remove the lid and check the quails are done. Their legs should pull away easily from their bodies.

    Reduce the sauce a little more if you wish.

    Serve, a quail each, drizzled with their capers and juices, and a good crust of bread for mopping up the juices.

PORK IN ANCHOVY SAUCE

Vitello Tonnato (Sardinian style)

Franca's signature recipe uses pork instead of veal. It is truly Sardinian, to slip in some pig wherever possible. I have heard tales of this swap before, and having eaten it many times now, I can confirm it is a highly successful one – I always make the dish this way myself. It is rarer to find veal here, whereas pork is ubiquitous, as well as cheaper and (generally) more humane.

SERVES 4

1 lean loin of pork
3 carrots, scrubbed
8 small waxy potatoes
2 celery sticks
1 onion, peeled
1 bay leaf
few sprigs of parsley
2 teaspoons sea salt

For the mayonnaise

2 egg yolks
1 scant teaspoon salt
200 ml (6¾ fl oz/scant 1 cup) best-quality extra virgin olive oil
100 ml (3¼ fl oz/scant ½ cup) neutral oil (such as sunflower)
1 scant teaspoon red wine vinegar
1 tablespoon lemon juice

For the sauce

1 x quantity mayonnaise (see above)
1 teaspoon capers, plus extra to serve
100 g (3½ oz) tuna (this is 1 small tin, drained)
4 anchovies, plus extra to serve
squeeze of lemon juice (optional)
finely chopped basil, to serve

Put the pork, vegetables and aromatics (apart from the basil) in a deep saucepan. Cover completely with cold water add the salt and place over the heat. Bring to the boil and then simmer until the pork is just cooked. This will only take around 20 minutes, depending on your pork. Aim for an internal temperature of 60°C (140°F). Remove the pork and set aside to cool before placing in the fridge to chill for at least 30 minutes. If the vegetables are not cooked, continue cooking until they are. Once they are done, remove them and leave them to cool.

You can eat the potatoes alongside the tonnato, as a simple salad, dressed with oil, salt, vinegar and parsley. You can also cut the carrots into quarter lengths on the diagonal and use them to decorate your tonnato.

To make the mayonnaise, place the yolks in your mixer, blender or bowl. Add the salt and start whisking. Drizzle the oils in drop by drop until they emulsify, making sure the mixture is being continuously and vigorously mixed, whatever the method. Add the vinegar and a good squeeze of lemon. Mix and taste for seasoning. Add more acidity or salt according to your preference. If you like, dilute with a little cold water to make it runnier.

To make the sauce, blitz everything together in an electric mixer until it is as chunky or smooth as you like it – I prefer mine to have a little texture but not to be lumpy. Taste for seasoning and adjust accordingly. Let it down with a touch of the cooking liquid or some lemon juice (depending on your preference) until it is a runnier consistency.

Thinly slice the pork, drape on a platter then pour over the sauce and serve with anchovies and scattered with the basil.

174

ROAST SUCKLING PIG

Maialetto Arrosto

It's hard to give a recipe for this, as it's more of an event than a formula with measurements and methods, but it would be sacrilege to have a book of Sardinian food without *porcheddu*.

If you are lucky enough to be able to get hold of a suckling pig, then before anything (and unless you have a spit) check it fits in your oven. Otherwise you will be in all sorts of trouble. Next, check you have a roasting tray large enough to hold it. If you cannot find a 'small pig' – though some meat companies and butchers will sell them – good quality pork would be an acceptable substitute.

I have cooked this once, long ago, before my life in Sardinia, for a family Christmas instead of a turkey. It was traumatic, to say the least. It barely fit in our oven – its nose pressed plaintively against the glass door – and its ears caught alight during cooking.

The final result was, needless to say, delicious, but I wouldn't recommend undertaking this unless you have ample courage and equipment. If you have both of these, you're in luck, because the actual cooking is fairly easy. The truth is the meat is so tender, and the crispy skin and layers of fat provide such a perfect and protective cooking coffin, that it's hard to screw this up. Even if you forget about it and cook it for too long, the meat will probably still be meltingly soft.

SERVES MANY

1 suckling pig
sea salt
myrtle branches or bay leaves,
  to serve

Preheat the oven to 170°C (340°F/Gas 3).

Season your piglet all over, inside and out, with sea salt. Place it sitting, sphinx-like, in a roasting dish. Roast it for 3–4 hours, until the meat gives when prodded with a fork. Serve on a bed of myrtle for true Sardinian authenticity, or branches of fresh bay if you can't find it.

PORK COOKED IN MILK WITH CLOVES

Maiale al Latte

My mother's bread sauce is the stuff of dreams. Pale pillows of creamy sweetness, a translucent curl or two of silken onion, the spicy whisper of cloves. Always served in the same green French earthenware pot, alongside roast chicken. Obviously when I regale Luca with this fond memory, he's horrified with the idea of eating milky, soggy bread with roast meat.

Bread sauce does not exist in Italy, but rather than eating meat with a milky sauce, there is a tradition of cooking the meat in milk. Pork cooked in milk is a well-known and loved Italian classic, and Marcella Hazan's infamous bolognaise ragù advises cooking the mince in milk to tenderise and enrich it. Milk, when cooked like this, becomes sweet, nutty, faintly caramelised and almost cheesy. It's a little like eating meat with a sort of cheese-infused cream. The cooked milk curds have the same savoury caramel note as a good aged Parmesan.

Franca told me about a Sardinian recipe for pork cooked in milk with cloves. It's one she learnt from her mother-in-law, and I suspect it may have trickled down by way of northern Italy, where milk is more common in cooking. Nonna Titina also liked to cook her minestra in milk. Either way, I tried it and it reminded me of my mother's bread sauce. It has the same heady sweet, savoury and spicy mix. A happy meeting of my old home, and my new one. Luca can go whistle. This dish is very, very beige, but don't let that deter you, it is delicious.

SERVES 8

3 kg (6 lb 10 oz) boned pork shoulder, trimmed of extra fat
sea salt
4 cloves
3 tablespoons olive oil
40 g (1½ oz) butter
3 sprigs of sage
6 garlic cloves, peeled
3 bay leaves
1.5 litres (51 fl oz/6½ cups) whole (full-fat) milk
peeled zest of 2 lemons
wilted greens, to serve

Season the pork well all over with sea salt and stud it with the cloves.

In a large, deep, frying pan (skillet) over a medium high heat, brown the pork in the oil evenly on all sides.

In a deep casserole dish (Dutch oven) over a medium heat, warm the butter. Add the sage and the garlic and allow to cook for a few minutes until fragrant.

Add the bay leaves, milk and the lemon zest. Bring the whole lot up to a simmer, add the pork and place the lid on, partially askew, to allow the steam to escape, and leave to cook over a low heat for at least 3 hours, until the meat is meltingly tender, and gives when prodded with a fork.

Serve in slices, with extra sauce spooned over the top, and some wilted greens.

POACHED MUTTON AND VEGETABLES

Pecora e Verdure

I am not – in general – a lover of lamb, but I love this dish. It really could not be simpler, more humble, or more delicious. It is a two-stage recipe, with the Malloreddus with mutton broth and pecorino (page 125) forming the first course, and then the poached meat and vegetables becoming the second. It's best made with a good, flavoursome piece of mutton, but if you cannot get hold of it, then good-quality lamb or hogget will do.

FEEDS 3–4

1 x quantity Mutton stock
   and meat (page 125)
3 onions
2 sundried tomatoes
3 small potatoes, peeled

Make the stock and meat according to page 125.

Once you have decanted enough broth to cook the pasta dish, add an extra 200 ml (6¾ oz/¾ cup) water to the pot with the mutton along with the onions, tomatoes and potatoes. Bring back to a simmer, cover, and cook for 20–30 minutes, until the vegetables are completely soft.

Serve the meat, onions and potatoes with the broth, for everyone to help themselves.

BROTH AND SOUP

Brodo e Minestra

I never really appreciated broth until I moved here. Growing up in England, we occasionally had stock at home, but it was always used as an ingredient to make a thick gravy for the Sunday roast, and I never thought about it beyond that.

Brodo in Italy is a world unto itself. Perhaps because poaching or boiling meat seems to be so much more a part of Italian cuisine than English. The only boiled meat I ate growing up was my grandmother's boiled ham. In England we seem to like our meat roasted, not boiled. At least my family did. Here, I am constantly given cuts of meat from the family labelled simply '*brodo*'. I don't even know what animal they came from, which is part of the fun. Poaching meat with vegetables, water and aromatics is an underrated cooking method. You can plonk everything in a saucepan, cover it with water and forget about it. The meat is rendered soft and juicy, and you also have a ready-made sauce, or broth, to serve with it. It is a true one-pot-wonder.

The ever-frugal Sardinians take this one step further. Not only do you have two distinct elements (in fact three, if we count the poached vegetables, the soft meat, and the clear broth), you also have two separate dishes and courses. The first plate is minestra. This is eaten as a pasta course. The clear broth is strained and pasta cooked inside it. It is then served in a bowl with grated Parmesan to add as you wish. The second (main) course is then the poached meat, soft and giving, and the poached vegetables, which have absorbed all of the flavour of the meat. I like to eat this with a little mayonnaise and some crusty bread. This ritualistic two-course meal is eaten at least once a week in our family, and is close to being my favourite meal of all. The flavours, colours and textures are pure comfort.

The thing that really distinguishes Sardinian poaching is their use of sundried tomatoes. Adding these to your broth gives it a rounded acidity and depth. Try and find the ones dried or packed in salt (which need a good rinsing first) rather than those in oil. As is true of so many of the best things, it is hard to give an exact recipe for making broth. Instead, I have the following guidance:

The length of cooking and the amount of water you add depends on which type of meat you are poaching, or what broth you are making.

BASIC BROTH

The constants are the vegetables that make up the broth base. For the following broths you will need:

1 carrot, peeled
1 large waxy potato, peeled
2 sundried tomatoes
1 celery stick, washed
1 small white onion, peeled

Put everything in a stock pot with the meat of your choice and follow the instructions below.

BEEF OR LAMB BROTH

For 500 g (1 lb 1¾ oz) beef or lamb (ask for slow-cooking cuts such as brisket, shoulder or rump) you will need 2 litres (68 fl oz/8 cups) water. This meat is tougher and so will take longer to cook. Simmer over a medium heat for around 1 hour or more, until the meat is tender.

Add salt to taste.

Now you will have soft, delicious vegetables, and tender, juicy meat for your second course, and clear, flavoursome broth for your first.

CHICKEN BROTH

For 500 g (1 lb 1¾ oz) chicken, whole or in pieces, you will need around 1.5 litres (51 fl oz/6½ cups) water. The chicken cooks quicker than red meat – usually taking around 30 minutes or less, and thus less of the liquid evaporates, so if you have huge amounts of water to begin with your broth will still be flavourless (diluted) even when the chicken is cooked. If you carry on cooking (to reduce the liquid) the chicken will dry out. It's a delicate balance.

MINESTRA

Now you've made the broth, you can prepare the minestra for the first course.

You will need 2 tablespoons of tiny, minestra-style pasta, such as risone, puntine or stelline, and 'two for the pot' (see note) for every 2 large ladles of broth. Bring the broth to the boil in a small saucepan and add the pasta – it might vary a little depending on the type, so check the package, but it should take around 6 minutes to cook.

Serve ladled in bowls, and sprinkle with grated Parmesan. Eat, with plenty of crusty bread, followed by the poached meat and vegetables with homemade Mayonnaise (page 174) or Aioli (page 69).

NOTE

Franca says you must put two extra spoonfuls for the pot *'due per la pentola'*. It reminds me of my father making tea for us at home; he always put in 'an extra bag for the pot'. It's a phrase that makes me happy.

SIX

MARE

Giuseppe's Marinated Salmon • Fish Fry with Saffron Aioli • Baby Octopus in Tomato Sauce • Grilled Octopus and Lemon Potato Purée • Braised Cuttlefish and Peas • Bream Baked with Potatoes • Roasted Stuffed Squid • Rock Lobster, Catalan Style

MARE

Fishing is a relatively new industry to Sardinia. Throughout its history, Sardinia became so used to sea-born invaders that her people migrated inland (hence the strong sheep-farming tradition). The turquoise waters that surround the island remained unfished until fairly recently. There is now a strong fishing tradition and some of the finest fish the Mediterranean has to offer.

Grey mullet is particularly common in our area. They are eaten boiled or grilled, and highly prized. Bass, snapper and bream are also common, as are squid, octopus, mussels, clams and prawns (shrimp).

When cooking a whole fish, it is best to get the freshest and best you can. Fresh fish should smell of nothing other than the sea and have bright-red gills and shining eyes. If cooking with shellfish, especially in pasta sauces etc., it is useful to have a store in the freezer. Sards use them often and the quality (and price) are usually good.

GIUSEPPE'S MARINATED SALMON

Salmone au Profumi d'Agrumi

Though originally (and rather grandly) named 'salmon perfumed with citrus', this has become known simply as 'Giuseppe's salmon'.

Giuseppe is not often to be found in the kitchen, unless it's to help himself to a chunk of cheese or a slice of salami, a trail of crumbs and some curls of cheese rind the tell-tale sign that he has been about. This is his signature (and possibly his only) dish, and very good it is, too. I have no idea where he got it from, but I like the element of mystery, which is heightened by his ritualistic style of making it (alone, unwatched).

It's a delicious and delicate way to start any meal.

FEEDS 10

1 whole side of salmon, deboned and skin on
1.5 kg (3 lb 5 oz) sea salt
400 g (14 oz) caster (superfine) sugar
handful of wild fennel fronds, roughly chopped (if you cannot source these use a chopped fennel bulb with plenty of its leaves intact), plus extra to serve
1 large lemon
1 large orange
best-quality olive oil, for drizzling
pink peppercorns, to serve

Choose a deep roasting tin large enough to fit the salmon. Inside it, place a small rack to sit the salmon on (it is important that the salmon is elevated so excess water can drip out of it whilst it cures). Mix the salt and sugar with the fennel fronds and place just over half of this mix over the salmon like a white crystal blanket. Chop the lemon and orange into small chunks and squeeze them over this. Then lay them on top of the salt-mound and cover with the rest of the salt-sugar mix. Put another roasting tin or baking (cookie) sheet on top of this and weigh down with something heavy. Leave in the fridge for 9–12 hours.

Remove the fish from the tin and shake off the salt. Rinse the fillet gently and then dry well with kitchen paper.

To serve, slice thinly and drizzle with your best olive oil, a smattering of pepper of your choice (pink pepper looks good) and some fronds of wild fennel.

FISH FRY WITH SAFFRON AIOLI

Fritto Misto con Aioli Zafferano

The classic Italian fish fry, which is no less loved in Sardinia. In fact, this dish is so loved that at most Sardinian weddings you will have a stand devoted to serving up paper cones of fresh fried goodies, to soak up the free-flowing prosecco.

For an authentic touch, serve this either in paper cones, or on paper squares.

SERVES 6 AS A STARTER

100 g (3½ oz) semolina
100 g (3½ oz) plain
  (all-purpose) or 00 flour
good pinch of sea salt, plus
  extra to serve
400 g (14 oz) squid, cleaned
  and cut into pieces
200 g (7 oz) prawns (shrimp),
  shells removed
200 g (7 oz) small frying
  fish, such as small mullet,
  whitebait or mangiatutti
1.5 litres (51 fl oz/6½ cups)
  neutral oil, for deep frying
lemon wedges, to serve
1 x quantity Saffron aioli
  (page 69)

Heat your frying oil to 190°C (375°F). See page 86 for notes on frying.

Have a vessel lined with kitchen paper ready beside you.

In a large bowl, mix the semolina and the flour together with the salt, and drop your fish into it. Toss them to make sure they are evenly coated in flour. Using a large sieve, fish(!!) them out, shake off any excess flour, drop them in the oil and fry until golden and crisp.

Remove with a slotted spoon and drain on the kitchen paper. Sprinkle with a little sea salt and serve, immediately, with lemon wedges and a pot of the saffron aioli.

BABY OCTOPUS IN TOMATO SAUCE

Moscardini alla Diavola

A lot of my favourite things are 'devilled'. Some of my granny's most notorious recipes were devilled kidneys and devilled crab. I was very happy to discover this Sardinian devil with *moscardini*, a tiny baby octopus. Here they are usually found frozen and braised in a tomato sauce spiked with chilli. I find they are best eaten on a bed of soft polenta.

If you cannot find baby octopus or moscardini, then a normal octopus will do, just make sure to cook it a little longer. You will also need to prep it and cut it into small pieces (page 198). Moscardini come ready to go, which is another point in their favour.

I like to serve a little gremolata on top of this, for some freshness and punch. Gremolata is basically finely chopped garlic, parsley and lemon zest, which can be used for garnishing any braise.

SERVES 6

3 garlic cloves, finely sliced
4 tablespoons olive oil
2 bay leaves
2 dried red chillies, chopped
1 kg (2 lb 3¼ oz) moscardini
   or octopus
250 ml (8½ fl oz/1 cup)
   Vernaccia or another dry
   white wine
800 g (1 lb 12¼ oz) tinned
   tomatoes, puréed (either
   with a stick blender
   or through a mouli)

For the gremolata

1 bunch fresh flat-leaf
   parsley, chopped
zest of 1 lemon, chopped
1 garlic clove, chopped

In a large frying pan (skillet) over a medium heat, fry the garlic in the oil until fragrant. Add the bay and chillies, stir for a minute or two and then add the octopus.

Cook for a few minutes and add the wine and the tomatoes.

Leave at a low simmer for around 1 hour, partially covered, stirring occasionally, until the octopus is completely tender.

While the moscardini is cooking, make the gremolata. Mix the ingredients together, tip onto a chopping board and then chop everything together until you have a fine sprinkle-able garnish.

Once the octopus is ready, serve immediately with the gremolata sprinkled on top.

GRILLED OCTOPUS AND LEMON POTATO PURÉE

Polpo Grigliato con Puré di Patate al Limone

Octopus is delicious twice-cooked. First boiled and then grilled, its sweet meatiness absorbs chargrilled flavour beautifully. Married with this sharp and silky potato purée, it makes a delicious and unusual combination. One of Luca's signature recipes.

When buying octopus, it is best to buy it frozen and then defrost it ready for cooking. Frozen octopus is ready to cook, and has already been tenderised, whilst fresh octopus needs a good bashing with a mallet to make it tender. The latter does, however, have its therapeutic qualities.

Both the purée and the octopus can be cooked in advance and reheated at the last moment.

SERVES 6

For the octopus

2 celery sticks, cut in half
1 onion, peeled
2 strips of lemon zest
2 dried red chillies
A handful of parsley stalks
1 medium-sized octopus

For the lemon potato purée

600 g (1 lb 5 oz) waxy
   yellow potatoes
130 ml (4½ fl oz) best-quality
   extra virgin olive oil
zest and juice of 1 large lemon
sea salt

To serve

dried red chillies
handful flat leaf
   parsley, chopped

First, prepare the octopus, or ask your fishmonger to do this for you. This can be done a day or two in advance if you like. Rinse it well under cold water, making sure any sand still stuck in the tentacles is removed. Cut away the eyes from the head, and wipe away anything from inside the hood of the head too. Cut out the beak from the base of the tentacle – there is a small round ball where the mouth parts are. Now place the octopus in a large saucepan with the other ingredients and fill the saucepan with cold water. The octopus must be completely submerged.

Bring the whole lot to the boil and then turn down to a simmer. Cook, half covered, for 1 hour or more, until the octopus is tender. Poke a tentacle with a sharp knife; if it sinks in easily, the octopus is cooked. Remove it from its crimson bath and leave it to cool.

Now make your potato purée. Peel, halve and boil your potatoes in plenty of salted water until completely soft.

Drain them and then blitz them into a purée using a stick blender or any other blender. They will look very gluey. Add the oil, lemon zest and juice and stir to combine. Add 4 tablespoons water and stir gently. They should no longer be gluey. Now you should have a smooth purée. Taste and season with more salt if necessary. It should be sharp and punchy from the oil and lemon.

Place a griddle pan on the heat or turn on your grill. Slice the tentacles off the octopus and place them in the hot griddle pan, or under the grill (broiler). Grill (broil) for a few moments on each side, then season with olive oil, salt, and some dried chilli. Place them on a dish of your warmed purée and serve, drizzled with extra oil and sprinkled with chilli and parsley.

BRAISED CUTTLEFISH AND PEAS

Seppie con Piselli

A simple and surprisingly good combination, and another reason to love frozen peas. The peas are cooked low and slow alongside the cuttlefish, ensuring both become meltingly tender and sweet.

There is a beach shack at Is Arutas, one of the famous beaches on the west coast near us in Oristano, where I first ate a version of this dish. The sand here is glittering quartz crystal. The sea is impossibly turquoise, set against the polished mahogany of Sardinian sunbathers and the dazzling white sand; it's quite a sight. The shack serves a selection of fish antipasti for a small price, and diners sit in their sandy costumes and eat off plastic plates on gingham tablecloths. It feels exactly as summer in Sardinia should.

At the beach-side trattoria, this dish is always served at room temperature –it is usually swelteringly hot outside – with a glass of chilled red wine. In summer, serve it like this as a simple starter or light lunch. In winter, you can serve it piping hot with some polenta and grilled bread. Maybe even some Aioli (page 69) for good measure.

If you cannot find cuttlefish then squid will work just as well. I use a mixture of passata (as the sauce base) and whole tomatoes for a little texture and interest, but the dish is also fine with a 400 g (14 oz) tin of chopped tomatoes.

SERVES 6

1 kg (2 lb 3¼ oz) cuttlefish, either small or large
1 small white onion, finely diced
2 large garlic cloves, finely sliced
4 tablespoons extra virgin olive oil
3 bay leaves
1 fennel bulb, finely diced and fronds reserved to garnish
2 whole dried red chillies
large handful freshly chopped parsley
200 ml (6¾ fl oz/¾ cup) passata
200 ml (6¾ fl oz/¾ cup) Vernaccia or another dry white wine
150 g (5¼ oz) chopped ripe tomatoes (I like the small sweet datterini variety best, chopped in half lengthwise)
500 g (1 lb 1½ oz) small frozen peas
sea salt, to taste
zest and juice of ½ a lemon

First, prep your cuttlefish, or alternatively, you could ask your fishmonger to do this for you.

Pull the head from the body, then, holding the top of the body tube, press the pointed tail end of the body down against a chopping board and push down. The single bone should break through the skin. Remove this and discard.

Now remove the insides, being careful not to break the ink sac (the black pouch of ink). If this breaks it's not the end of the world, but things will get much messier. Remove and reserve the liver, which is pale brown and creamy looking. You can freeze this and cook it later, in other fishy braises or soups. Rinse the body tube and pull away the wings and most of the skin. Discard the skin but keep the thin wings, as these are cooked in the stew. Slice away the eyes and the beak of the cuttlefish, so that all you have remaining is the mass of tentacles, the two little wings, and the clean body tube. Slice these into even sized pieces.

In a large frying pan (skillet) over a low medium heat, cook the diced onion and the garlic in the olive oil. Add the bay leaves, diced fennel and chillies and cook on a gentle heat until the onion is translucent and just beginning to turn golden (this will take at least 20 minutes). Add the cuttlefish and half of the chopped parsley and cook for a few minutes. Now add the passata, wine and tomatoes. Simmer until the cuttlefish is tender – it is hard to give an exact time for this, but it will take either a little under or a little over 1 hour. When the cuttlefish is just tender, add the peas and cook for another 10–15 minutes, until they too are sweet and tender. Taste and add salt if necessary. Add the lemon zest and juice and stir. Serve, garnished with the rest of the chopped parsley and the fennel fronds.

BREAM BAKED WITH POTATOES

Orata al Forno con Patate

A classic all over Italy, I like to make this as a sort of alternative Sunday roast. It makes a wonderful centrepiece and encourages the sort of communal, finger-sucking, bread-dunking atmosphere that makes for the most enjoyable weekend lunches.

It is also remarkably delicious for something so simple and tastes like a refined version of fish and chips.

I vary what I add to it according to what I have at home. Sometimes a sprig of rosemary, sometimes some sliced fennel or mushrooms. Often if I don't have tomatoes (or it's not the season) I leave them out. It's good any which way. It's important to be generous with the oil.

SERVES 4

500 g (1 lb 1½ oz) potatoes
sea salt
best-quality olive oil
handful of cherry tomatoes
  (optional)
handful of green olives
  (optional)
handful of parsley, very
  roughly chopped
1 small glass of Vernaccia
  or another dry white wine
2 garlic cloves, halved
1 large bream

Preheat the oven to 200°C (400°F/Gas 6).

Wash the potatoes but don't bother peeling them. Slice them into thin discs – as thin as you can manage without wasting time and worrying about it.

Lay the potato slices in a roasting tin or gratin dish and season well with salt. Add a hefty glug of olive oil and stir them around with your hands until they are all well coated and oily.

Tear the tomatoes in and scatter them about.

Sprinkle over the olives and the parsley, add the wine and the garlic cloves. Arrange everything evenly and flatly, like a nicely made bed ready to receive the fish.

Season the fish well with salt and drizzle with some oil.

Place it on top of its bed and put the tin in the oven.

Cook for around 30 minutes, until the fish is done. If your potatoes are still a little *al dente* but the fish is done, remove the fish, set aside and cover with foil, and return the potatoes to the oven for a few more minutes.

Serve on the table in the roasting tin for people to serve themselves.

ROASTED STUFFED SQUID

Calamari Ripieni

I love squid, but am always stumped when it comes to trying new recipes with it, and tend to fall back on simply chargrilling or frying it. This is a brilliant recipe – another of Franca's staples – substantial enough to be a main course, and highly adaptable, too.

SERVES 4

8 medium squid
2 garlic cloves, peeled
   and halved
5 tablespoons olive oil
300 ml (10 fl oz/1¼ cups)
   white wine
large handful of parsley,
   chopped
good pinch of dried red chilli
handful of fresh basil, chopped
160 g (5½ oz/generous 1 cup)
   breadcrumbs
6 anchovies, minced
40 g (1½ oz) Parmesan, grated
6 anchovies, minced
squeeze of lemon juice and
   a little grated zest
sea salt, to taste
tomato salad or green salad,
   to serve

Clean the squid. Start by gently pulling the head away from the body and removing the 'quill', the see-through backbone. Cut away the eyes and the beak from the tentacles and discard them. Pull away the wings from the body tube and rinse inside the tube.

Chop the wings and the tentacles into tiny pieces and reserve the tubes.

In a large frying pan (skillet) over a medium heat, cook the garlic in half of the oil until it just becomes fragrant. Remove the garlic and discard. Add the small, chopped squid pieces and cook until just beginning to turn golden, around 2–3 minutes. Add 100 ml (3½ fl oz/scant ½ cup) of the wine to the pan, and cook for a further minute or two until reduced then take off the heat.

Decant the squid pieces and their juices into a mixing bowl and stir in the parsley, chilli, basil, breadcrumbs, anchovies and Parmesan. Add the lemon juice and zest and mix well. Taste for seasoning, adding more salt if necessary.

Hold open the cleaned body tubes and stuff them full of the stuffing. Skewer them closed with two toothpicks and set aside until you are ready to cook them.

Place the remaining olive oil in a wide lidded frying pan (it needs to accommodate all your squid) and set over a medium heat. Add the squid and brown them evenly on all sides. Add the remainder of the wine and cover with a lid, turning the heat down a little. Cook for 10 minutes or so until the squid are tender.

Serve, drizzled with their juices, with a tomato or green salad alongside.

NOTE

If I'm making this dish in the summer, I add a very ripe tomato or two to the pot when I am cooking the whole stuffed squid, just before adding the wine. Then I serve it with some torn basil and bruschetta rubbed with garlic and drizzled with oil.

ROCK LOBSTER, CATALAN STYLE

Aragosta alla Catalana

Aragosta are Sardinian rock lobsters that are usually caught off the western coast. This dish is a speciality of Alghero, a city an hour or so north of Oristano, and an inheritance of the Catalan invaders.

If you cannot find rock lobsters, this is also very good with any other type of lobster.

In Oristano, this is a once-a-year type of dish, but it's almost always the best day of the year; saved for high summer and favourite guests or family.

We traipse down to the beach to collect sea water in big plastic containers to cook our lobsters in, and Luca begins his annual 'Sardinian sea water is the purest, saltiest sea water in the *world*' lecture as we carry it back to the house.

SERVES 4

a few litres of finest Sardinian sea water (or realistically, well sea-salted tap water)
2 live rock lobsters
juice of ½ a lemon
sea salt
100 ml (3½ fl oz/scant ½ cup) best-quality olive oil
1 small red onion, finely sliced
2½ tablespoons red wine vinegar
handful of fresh basil, torn, plus whole leaves to serve
handful of fresh parsley, shredded
500 g (1 lb 1½ oz) best, ripest tomatoes, chopped into chunks

Fill a large, deep saucepan with your water (whether from tap or sea) and bring it to the boil.

Lower in the first of your lobsters, and cover with a lid. Boil for 8 minutes. Remove with a slotted spoon, set aside to cool, and repeat with the next.

When the lobsters have cooled, cut them in half lengthways. Remove the liver (the pale green or beige creamy mass inside the head cavity). Mix this with the lemon, a pinch of salt, and half of the oil to make a simple dressing.

In a small bowl, soak the onion slices in half of the vinegar for 10 minutes to remove some of their sharpness. Drain. Mix the onion, herbs and tomatoes in a bowl then scatter over a serving platter and set aside.

When the lobster is completely cold and you are ready to eat, cut each half into chunks (you can either use a mallet and keep the shell on here, which is visually more striking, or you remove all the meat from the shell).

Marinate these chunks in the remaining vinegar, another pinch of salt, the rest of the olive oil and the dressing. Toss well, making sure all of the meat is coated.

Pour the dressed meat over the tomatoes and herbs, making sure to drizzle the remaining dressing over the top. Scatter over some whole basil leaves, drizzle with a little more oil and serve, preferably with a bottle of chilled prosecco.

SEVEN

DOLCI E BEVANDE

Saffron Custard and Panettone Pudding • Two-Booze Tiramisu
• *Bittersweet* • Fried Ravioli with Cheese and Honey • Almond
Panna Cotta with Rose Poached Cherries and Wild Fennel • Olive
Oil Ice Cream with Seville Orange • Campari and Blood Orange
Granita • Watermelon and Mint Granita • Apricot and Amaretti
Crumble with Vanilla Mascarpone Cream • Chocolate Orange
Mascarpone Mousse with Poached Kumquats • Theresa's
Mandarin and Lemon Liqueurs • *As Red as the Devil Himself*

DOLCI E BEVANDE

Meals in Sardinia always culminate in fresh fruit, whatever is in season, and occasionally this may be followed by *dolci* (sweets).

Dolci are not designed to be 'pudding' or dessert, as such, in fact, they are entirely different beasts: light, sweet morsels eaten after the fruit with the coffee. More like *petit fours*.

Here, they are generally sweet little cakes, tarts or biscuits, mostly made with ingredients that are readily available, such as almonds, sugar and lemon. Occasionally they may be flavoured with vanilla or saffron, but though there are endless varieties, the overall theme tends to revolve around these flavours and textures.

Few Sardinians still make dolci at home – they tend to be bought from local bakeries. Every Saturday and Sunday in Oristano, you will see Sardinians en route to a meal wielding a cardboard tray wrapped in paper; a selection of dolci to offer as a gift.

Apart from tiramisu (page 216) and panna cotta (page 222), which one does still encounter everywhere, the sweet recipes in this book are mostly of my own invention, and are not traditionally Sardinian as such – rather a sort of English-pudding spin inspired by ingredients prevalent over here. I've fed them to (initially) sceptical Sardinians, who have loved them. I guess the proof really is in the pudding.

SAFFRON CUSTARD AND PANETTONE PUDDING

Budino di Panettone

The best thing about Christmas in Italy is panettone. This yeasty-sweet, brioche-style bread enriched with candied and dried fruit is one of my favourite things in the world. I love to eat great, soft fistfuls of it, as it is, and I love to use it in baking. The following buttercup-yellow, wobbling pudding is an Italianisation of one of my favourite English dishes, and just one of panettone's pleasure-giving possibilities.

Panettone should not be hard to find in England. Lidl stock it almost all year round, and theirs is usually Italian and very cheap. It is always on offer in supermarkets just after Christmas, too.

The bain marie method may seem like a faff, but it really does make for the best consistency, as I like my bread and butter pudding almost like a crème brûlée with pieces of bread in it, rather than totally solid. For me, it is as much about the custard as it is about the bread.

SERVES 6

250 g (8¾ oz) panettone,
    roughly half a large one
80 g (2¾ oz) butter
6 egg yolks
60 g (2 oz/¼ cup) caster
    (superfine) sugar
500 ml (17 fl oz/8 cups) whole
    (full-fat) milk
250 ml (8 fl oz/1 cup) double
    (heavy) cream, plus extra
    to serve
1 strip orange peel
pinch of saffron
4 tablespoons demerara sugar
marsala ice cream,
    to serve

Preheat the oven to 165°C (330°F/Gas 3).

Slice the panettone into 1.5 cm- (1 in-) thick slices. Unusually, I'm quite precise about this, as if the slices are too thick they soak up all the custard, and your finished pudding is too dry.

Making sure the butter is soft enough to spread, butter each slice of panettone well and lay in a medium gratin dish (the sort you would use for a lasagne) to make an even coating of two layers.

Whisk the yolks with the caster (superfine) sugar in a deep mixing bowl.

In a medium-sized saucepan, bring the milk and cream to the boil with the orange peel and saffron then take off the heat. Set aside for 1–2 minutes to infuse, and whilst still warm, strain the cream mixture into the yolks, whisking all the time.

Pour the custard slowly over the panettone, waiting a moment for it to be absorbed, then topping up any gaps. You want the solids to be totally submerged with a good 'float' of custard above, like a puddle of cream on porridge.

Sprinkle over the demerara and place the dish inside a large, deep roasting tin. Pour boiling water (from a kettle) halfway up the sides of the dish to make a bain marie. Cook for 35–45 minutes until golden brown and just set, with a slight wobble in the middle. Serve with double cream or marsala ice cream, if you can find it. This is best eaten, like many eggy dishes, after a little 10-minute pause to 'settle'.

TWO-BOOZE TIRAMISU

Tiramisu

A cliché it may be, but the Sards are no less fond of this 1950s Italian classic than I am, and I see no reason not to be, because when done well, it can be one of the nicest things to eat. Don't be put off by mediocre tiramisu experiences – this recipe is totally fool-proof, and I have fed it to many Sardinians, who declared it is the best they have ever tasted.

Literally translated as 'pick-me-up,' tiramisu is not only delicious as a dessert: it is the perfect thing for breakfast after a heavy night, the booze and coffee providing both the hair-of-the-dog and the caffeine necessary. There is no time of *any* day, in fact, when a little pick-me-up is not welcome.

For me the key is the quantity of alcohol. Like a good trifle, it is this boozy kick that elevates the childhood nostalgia of a custardy cream and cake combo into something a little more adult and refined.

I like to make mine in a big dish or trifle bowl for serving by the generous scoopful, rather than in individual portions. A traditional tiramisu has only two layers of biscuit, but you can scale this recipe up quite easily, or use a tall but narrow vessel, as I have done here, to create more layers.

FEEDS 4 GREEDY PEOPLE, OR 6 ASCETICS

3 eggs, separated
100 g (3½ oz/½ cup) caster (superfine) sugar
500 g (1 lb 1½ oz) mascarpone
200 ml (6¾ fl oz/¾ cup) strong black espresso coffee
80 ml (2¾ fl oz/⅓ cup) marsala
1½ tablespoons brandy
20–24 Savoiardi (ladyfinger) biscuits
5 tablespoons bitter cocoa powder, for dredging

Place the yolks and the sugar in a mixing bowl and whisk with an electric beater (or in a stand mixer) until they become thick, pale and mousse-like.

Mix in the mascarpone by hand, folding it in until completely incorporated.

In a small bowl, mix the coffee with the marsala and brandy.

Whisk the egg whites until smooth, creamy peaks are formed, but not too stiff so that they become dry. Fold into the mascarpone mixture, incorporating them gently so as not to lose too much air.

Dunk the Savoiardi briefly into the coffee mixture, making sure they are fully immersed, and arrange them on the base of your chosen serving bowl. The idea is not to have them either sopping or still-crisp, but somewhere in between. I dip, hold for a second, turn and hold for another second, and then remove. It pays to be diligent here, as no one wants a tiramisu swimming in liquid.

Scoop the first half of the mascarpone mixture over the biscuit layer. Spread out evenly. Repeat the soaked-Savoiardi layer and then finish with the second mascarpone layer on top of this. Dredge well with bitter cocoa powder and place in the fridge to set for at least an hour or two. If you like, you can add more cocoa powder just before serving, but I like it when it has slightly melted into the cream.

BITTERSWEET

Cooking, like life, is about balance, and the sweet is only defined as such by the presence of a contrasting bitter.

Bitterness is an important element in Sardinian dishes, and one of the things that appeals most to me in this cuisine. Almost all of my favourite things to eat or drink are a balance of the bitter and the sweet. Bitter-sweet Campari for aperitivo, bitter black coffee and a sugar-dusted pastry for breakfast, artichokes and marmalade, to name a few.

This bitter-sweetness is epitomised in one of the island's most feted and extraordinary products, *miele di corbezzolo*, after which this book is named.

Arbutus unedo (corbezzolo, or strawberry trees) grow wild all over Sardinia. They are evergreens with waxy, deep green leaves, and bell-like white blossoms which bloom in October and November. These blossoms turn into vivid red, ball-shaped berries, which vaguely resemble strawberries (hence the name). The flavour is faint and the texture a little mushy, but they are beautiful to look at. On the island, they are mostly made into liqueurs or jams rather than eaten as they are.

The name unedo derives from Pliny the Elder, who allegedly said of the fruit '*unum tantum ego*' ('I only eat one'). Whether he meant they were so good he could only allow himself one, or so uninteresting that he never wanted another remains unclear, but having tried them myself, I suspect the latter. The true beauty of this plant, aside from its aesthetics and the fact that it was Joni Mitchell's favourite tree, is the blossom, which the bees use to make honey.

Miele di corbezzolo is rare and prized. As the tree only blossoms for two months of the year, and is very susceptible to changes in weather, this honey is expensive and difficult to produce. It is also extremely labour-intensive for the Sardinian bees, who have to complete many trips from flower to hive to collect enough nectar. A standard honey requires a bee to make around 3,000 trips to and from home, but this type of honey requires 6,000–8,000. There is something rather special about knowing that this unusual honey is the product of hard work and serious dedication.

Most of this honey is produced in Barbagia, in the mountains around Nuoro, thus named by the Romans after the barbarians that inhabited the area and until relatively recently, the area was still known for banditry. The honey can be found from some specialist suppliers, and its aroma of smoky coffee and wild herbs makes it wonderful with cheese. It is also the perfect honey to serve with Seadas (page 221).

FRIED RAVIOLI WITH CHEESE AND HONEY

Seadas

Also known as *Sebadas*, this is Sardinia's most iconic dessert.

These pastries are a celebration of the simplicity and quality of Sardinian produce: more specifically, cheese and honey.

Traditionally a fresh pecorino is used, which is only aged for a few days and allowed to become slightly sour, then seasoned with lemon zest and encased in a lard-based pastry. The cheesy parcel is then deep-fried until it blisters and puffs and is served, golden and glistening, bathed in honey. Often the honey is the famous *miele di corbezzolo*, which has a slight bitter-sweetness; a chestnut honey works well too.

If you dislike lard, you can use olive oil or butter, and if you can't find fresh pecorino, try to find a fresh sheeps', goats' or cows' cheese. What is important is that it is rubbery rather than creamy, as this is what gives it the stringy texture when melted.

MAKES 4

For the pastry

pinch of sea salt
100 g (3½ oz/¾ cup) 00 flour, plus 1 tablespoon for the filling
100 g (3½ oz/¾ cup) semolina
20 g (¾ oz) lard, at room temperature

For the filling

260 g (9 oz) fresh pecorino, cut into small pieces
zest of 1 lemon
sea salt (optional)
sunflower oil, for deep-frying
honey, for drizzling

Add the salt and 100 ml (3½ fl oz/scant ½ cup) water to the flour and semolina and knead together to form a smooth dough. Now knead in the lard. This should take a good few minutes of steady kneading.

Wrap in cling film (plastic wrap) and rest for 30 minutes.

Melt the cheese very gently in a bain marie. When it starts to form one gooey mass, add a spoonful of flour to soak up the liquid that has seeped out. Stir gently and add the lemon zest – if using fresh pecorino, add a pinch of salt here too if you like.

When the cheese mixture has come together into one melty mass, tip it onto a clean baking (cookie) sheet, spread in into an even layer 1 cm (½ in) thick, and leave to cool and set.

Meanwhile, roll out your pastry to 1 mm thickness, using either flour or semolina if it gets sticky. Cut circles using a biscuit cutter, around the size of a large orange or small grapefruit.

Using a smaller cutter or a glass tumbler if you don't have one, cut smaller circles of the cheese; by now it should be solid.

Place the circle of cheese in the centre of the circles of dough. Brush around them with a damp pastry brush. Place another circle of pastry on top to sandwich the cheese, and then press down to form little parcels. Seal them well (I cut them into circles again at this point using a ravioli cutter to get nice, even, crinkly edges).

Place on baking sheet lined with baking paper and keep in the fridge or freezer until ready to serve.

When you are ready to cook, bring your oil to frying temperature, 190°C (375°F). Delicately place the seadas in the oil and fry them until they are golden and crisp. Fish them out with a slotted spoon and drain them quickly on kitchen paper. Serve, drizzled with honey.

ALMOND PANNA COTTA WITH ROSÉ POACHED CHERRIES AND WILD FENNEL

Panna Cotta di Mandorle, Ciliegie e Finocchietto Selvatico

Panna cotta is a wonderfully gentle, creamy way to finish a meal. It couldn't be easier to make.

There are some lovely rosé wines made in Sardinia, and whilst I rarely drink them, I like cooking with them. They work particularly well with fruit. The gentle flavour of the almonds is cool and luxurious in a pale, wobbling panna cotta. The wild fennel highlights the delicate anise flavours of the cherry and wine, but if you cannot find it then chervil is a good substitute.

SERVES 6

200 g (7 oz) whole
  peeled almonds
550 ml (18½ fl oz/2 cups)
  single (light) cream
3 strips of lemon zest
80 g (2¾ oz/⅓ cup) caster
  (superfine) sugar
2 gelatine leaves

To serve

300 g (10½ oz) cherries
1 glass of rosé wine
100 g (3½ oz/½ cup) caster
  (superfine) sugar
zest and juice of ½ lemon
  fronds of wild fennel
  or chervil, to serve

Set the oven to 170°C (340°F/Gas 3). Roast the almonds until they just begin to smell nutty, for about 8–10 minutes. Once they've cooled a little, roughly chop.

In a small saucepan, bring the chopped almonds, cream, lemon zest and sugar to the boil then simmer very gently, stirring occasionally and allowing the almonds to seep their flavours into the mix. After a few minutes, remove from the heat and set aside.

In the meantime, soak the gelatine in a bowl of cold water. When it is totally soft, add it to the warm mixture and stir well. The gelatine should dissolve completely (if it doesn't, warm the whole mix a little again). Strain through a fine sieve into a pouring jug. You can keep the almonds to add to your porridge or muesli the next day).

Divide your mixture into ramekins or serving dishes of your choice. Chill in the fridge until set, around 3–4 hours. If eating the next day, cover well and remove from the fridge an hour or so before you want to eat them.

Stone and halve the cherries. Place them in a shallow pan with the wine, a splash of water, sugar and lemon zest. Cover. Bring to a simmer and then poach until the cherries are soft but not mushy, around 10–15 minutes. Taste the sauce and reduce to your taste, adding more lemon juice or sugar to your liking. Allow to cool.

When ready to serve, spoon the cherries on top of the panna cottas and scatter with the fennel or chervil.

OLIVE OIL ICE CREAM WITH SEVILLE ORANGE ZEST

Gelato all'Olio di Oliva con Arancia di Siviglia

My love of olive oil knows no bounds, it's true, but this is utter genius and not a gimmick. The oil lends a smooth and rounded lusciousness to the ice cream and, seeing as olive oil goes well with chocolate, nuts and fruit, this ice cream pairs beautifully with puddings based around any of these (which is most puddings). Here I have paired it with the wonderfully aromatic zest of Seville oranges. If you cannot get hold of these (they are in season in January, but freeze well) then a mandarin will do.

SERVES 6

4 egg yolks
200 g (7 oz/1 cup) caster (superfine) sugar
500 ml (17 fl oz/2 cups) double (heavy) cream
250 ml (8 fl oz/1 cup) whole (full-fat) milk
pinch of sea salt
60 ml (2 fl oz/¼ cup) best-quality, fruity olive oil, plus extra to serve
zest of 1 Seville orange

Using an electric whisk, mix the yolks with the sugar until pale and mousse-like.

In a saucepan over a medium heat, warm the cream and milk until they just comes to a simmer then pour over the yolks in a steady stream, whisking all the time. Return the mixture to a clean pan and cook over a low heat, stirring continuously, until the custard begins to thicken, enough to coat the back of a wooden spoon. If you like, you can use a thermometer to check this, it should read around 72°C (162°F).

Add the pinch of salt.

Strain the custard through a fine sieve into a wide bowl and chill for at least 4 hours, but preferably overnight. When chilled, remove from the fridge and whisk in the olive oil (I use a stick blender for this) until completely emulsified. Churn in an ice-cream machine and freeze.

Serve with freshly grated Seville orange zest and an extra drizzle of oil.

CAMPARI AND BLOOD ORANGE GRANITA

Granita al Campari e Arancia Sanguigna

Campari is almost always served with an accompanying slice of orange. The aromatics from the skin of the orange enhance those in the Campari, and it is also delicious drunk with the juice of the orange itself. This combination makes one of my favourite granitas. Just as a Campari rejuvenates the palate before eating, so it refreshes it afterwards, and this sorbet is the perfect end to a spring or summer meal.

Blood oranges vary wildly in flavour, so it is essential that you taste this and adjust the sweetness accordingly.

In this recipe, I used the premixed Campari soda, because we always have them in the fridge. If you can't find them, then substitute it for 4 tablespoons of pure Campari.

SERVES 4

150 g (5¼ oz/¾ cup) caster
   (superfine) sugar
finely grated zest of 1 blood
   orange
1 small bottle of Campari
   Soda (100 ml/3½ fl oz)
400 ml (13½ fl oz/1¾ cups)
   blood orange juice, strained
juice 1 lemon

In a small saucepan over a low heat, mix the sugar with the grated zest and the Campari, stirring until it has dissolved. Bring to the boil and boil for 2 minutes then remove from the heat.

Pour the blood orange juice into the syrup, mix well and add the lemon juice. Taste for seasoning.

Pour into a shallow container and freeze, removing it a couple of times after an hour or two to scrape with a fork (see additional note on granita, page 229).

WATERMELON AND MINT GRANITA

Granita all'Anguria e Menta

There are only so many times you can serve iced, sliced watermelon to your guests during high summer in Sardinia. It's all anybody really wants to eat, but it does become a bit monotonous. At this time of year, the melons are at their best, and your cooking is at its worst; by that I mean that dragging yourself damply into the kitchen to do anything more involved than slicing a fruit is painstaking. This granita is as refreshing (if not more so) and delicious as a chilled slice of watermelon, and only a little more effort.

I like it very sharp so add lots of lemon but depending on the sweetness of your melon – and your palate – you may want to adjust.

SERVES 6

150 g (5¼ oz/¾ cup) caster
   (superfine) sugar
4 sprigs of mint, washed
   and patted dry
1 medium watermelon, plus
   extra slices to serve
juice of 4 lemons

In a small saucepan, bring 200 ml (6¾ oz/¾ cup) water and the sugar to the boil and simmer for a few minutes until syrupy.

Remove from the heat and leave to cool. Add 3 of the 4 mint sprigs, stir and leave to infuse. Strain when cool.

In a blender, blitz the watermelon flesh with the plucked leaves from the remaining mint sprig and strain the mixture through a fine sieve. Add the watermelon juice to the strained sugar syrup along with the lemon juice to the watermelon, tasting as you go.

Pour into a shallow container and put in the freezer. Mash it up with a fork every time you think of it. Allow at least 7 hours (depending on your freezer) before it is frozen. Serve in dainty glasses with a slice of fresh melon on the side.

APRICOT AND AMARETTI CRUMBLE WITH VANILLA MASCARPONE CREAM

Budino di Albicocca e Amaretti con Crema di Mascarpone

This is an invention born of necessity, based around ingredients that are prevalent here in Sardinia, to satisfy my British crumble cravings.

The apricot is related to the almond, so the two sit happily side by side in this ensemble.

The vanilla mascarpone cream is really a sort of mousse. If you like, you can set it in the fridge and serve with biscuits and a glass of sweet wine as a simple pudding.

SERVES 6

850 g (1 lb 14 oz) ripe apricots,
  halved and destoned
80 g (2¾ oz/scant ½ cup)
  caster (superfine) sugar
zest and juice of 1 large lemon

For the topping

120 g (4¼ oz/1 cup) plain
  (all-purpose) flour
120 g (4¼ oz) unsalted butter
50 g (1¾ oz/¼ cup)
  demerara sugar
100 g (3½ oz) amaretti biscuits
70 g (2½ oz/⅔ cup)
  flaked almonds
pinch of sea salt

*For the vanilla
mascarpone cream*

3 eggs, separated
1 vanilla pod, seeds scraped
90 g (3¼ oz/scant ½ cup)
  caster (superfine) sugar
500 g (1 lb 1¾ oz) marscarpone

Preheat the oven to 190C (375°F/Gas 5).

In a saucepan over a medium heat, mix the apricots with the sugar, lemon zest and juice and a splash of water and cook until just collapsing and starting to become jammy, about 15 minutes. You want a good juicy apricot gravy here, which is essential to bubble over the rubble of the crumble. If your fruit is unripe and hard this may take a while, and you may have to add more sugar or lemon or water accordingly. Taste as you go. Pour the apricots into a large gratin dish and set to one side.

Put the flour, butter, sugar, amaretti, and two thirds of the flaked almonds into a mixer and blitz until a camel-brown rubble is formed; you can do this by hand just by rubbing the butter into the flour with your fingers and then adding the amaretti, crushed beforehand with a rolling pin. It is best if the rubble is uneven, with some pieces a little larger than others. Uniformity is not what you're aiming for.

Place your crumble mix in the freezer for 20 minutes – this ensures the perfect crumble texture.

Pour the mixture over the waiting fruit in its dish and sprinkle the top with the remaining flaked almonds and salt. Bake for about 30 minutes, until golden and bubbling.

While the crumble is baking, make the mascarpone cream. Beat the yolks, vanilla seeds and sugar until pale and fluffy. Add the mascarpone and beat until smooth. Beat the whites in a separate (clean) bowl until they form soft peaks and fold into the rest of the mixture until it is smooth. Chill in the fridge until ready for serving.

Serve the crumble with spoonfuls of the mascarpone cream.

CHOCOLATE ORANGE MASCARPONE MOUSSE WITH POACHED KUMQUATS

Mousse al Cioccolato con Mandarino Cinese Canditi

This is such an incredibly quick and simple mousse it beggars belief. No faffing about whisking egg whites and yolks. It's ready to serve within minutes and tastes absolutely delicious.

Kumquats and Seville oranges grow well in Sardinia, so well they are easy to forage from laden boughs drooping over garden walls. The flavour of Seville orange zest is the purest orange flavour you can find, but if you cannot find them then normal oranges will do.

SERVES 6

500 g (1 lb 1¾ oz) kumquats,
   chopped
150 g (5½ oz/¾ cup) caster
   (superfine) sugar

For the mousse

300 g (10½ oz) dark chocolate
2 eggs
zest of 1 Seville orange
500 g (1 lb 1¾ oz) mascarpone
4 tablespoons whole
   (full-fat) milk

First, make the kumquats. In a saucepan over a medium heat, bring the sugar and 150 ml (5½ fl oz/⅔ cup) water to the boil. Add the kumquats, cut according to your preference. Cook at a simmer for around 15 minutes, until completely tender and syrupy. Set aside to cool.

While the fruit is cooling, make the chocolate mousse. Melt the chocolate over a bain marie until completely liquid. Remove from the heat and stir in the eggs. It will start to look very thick and glossy.

Now whisk in the zest and the mascarpone. It will become a lovely mousse-like consistency.

Depending on your mascarpone, this mixture may become very thick quite quickly after you whisk it all together. I like my mousse a little silkier and softer, so at this stage I gently whisk in the milk, to let it down a little. Do as you see fit.

Serve in glasses immediately, with some of the kumquats spooned over the top.

THERESA'S MANDARIN AND LEMON LIQUEURS

Mandarinetto e limoncello

This is a recipe from Luca's great aunt Theresa, a woman both wonderful and terrifying in equal measure. She makes infamously good liqueurs with Sardinian citrus. She also dresses exclusively in fur coats, designer sunglasses and woollen berets, and was left at the altar by the (one) love of her life. As a result, she has sworn off men – and people in general – ever since. Liqueurs, after all, don't let you down.

These little glowing bottles make wonderful gifts. I make my own batch in January, when the citrus is at its best, and the weather is at its worst, as it's a good indoor activity. This way you can gift them throughout the year, and the following Christmas.

In Italian supermarkets they sell pure alcohol (96 per cent proof anyway) and the Sards always have a bottle on hand for impromptu liqueur making. As this is not available outside Italy, I have given the recipe as though a normal (40 per cent) vodka was being used.

You will need good, unwaxed, organic fruit for this, as the skins are infused, so if they are sprayed with chemicals it will affect the final result.

MAKES 1 LITRE OR ENOUGH FOR 4 SMALL, GIFT-SIZED BOTTLES

3 lemons or 8 mandarins, well washed
500 ml (17 fl oz/2 cups) alcohol
350 g (12 oz/1¾ cups) caster (superfine) sugar

Wash your fruit well in cold water.

Peel the lemons (or mandarins) using a swivel peeler, pressing only lightly to take the most superficial peel, and none of the white pith with it. The white pith will make your drink bitter, so it is important to be attentive here. It is not difficult with the lemon peel, but quite tiresome with the mandarin peel. If you choose large, firm mandarins it should be a little easier. After peeling off the strips, you can also cut away any remaining white pith with a small, sharp knife, pressing the strips down and cutting away from you.

Place the peel in a large, lidded, sterilized jar and pour over 250 ml (8½ fl oz/1 cup) the alcohol. Leave for 30 days to infuse.

After the 30 days is up, bring your infused mixture to the boil, simmer for a moment and then add 300 ml (10 fl oz/1¼ cups) water and the sugar. Stir to dissolve the sugar and simmer for another moment, then set aside and leave to cool completely.

Once cool, strain through a sieve, discarding the peel. Decant into bottles and keep in the freezer or fridge.

AS RED AS
THE DEVIL HIMSELF

in the night. With the glass in one dainty, manicured hand, they smoked cigarettes and ate salted crisps with the other. I was desperate to find out what that drink was, and to try it. I ordered one, and sure enough, salted crisps heralded its arrival, and I tried my first Campari soda. It was icy cold and bitter - so bitter, medicinal even. I almost hated it. But then I drank some more and ate some crisps, and the salt tempered it; slowly it became more palatable. By the time I finished it I had *almost* grown to like it and - as I was by now determined on my path - I ordered another.

Like olives, coffee and cigarettes, Campari takes a bit of getting used to. When I was young, I thought it was terribly sophisticated to eat olives, so I trained myself to like them. I felt the same about black coffee. As I grew older, my palate changed, and I grew to love the bitter flavour of both of these things, and not just to love them, but to crave them. I feel the same way about Campari now. It is the liquid epitome of bitter-sweetness, or *dolce amaro*. And as such, it is the perfect aperitif: it complements salty things, green olives or plain crisps, and it sharpens the senses and awakens the palate for what is to follow.

Campari is my chosen poison; bitter, pungent and shrouded in mystery. Developed by Gaspare Campari in 1860, the recipe remains a top secret, and the only two known ingredients are alcohol and water. The rest of this flame-red aperitif is made up of a secret combination of aromatic herbs and fruit.

Gaspare cooked up the special concoction in the back of his café-bar in Novara, and his wife, Letizia (my name-sake), later took over the business and ran it after his death. Perhaps no coincidence then, that I should have such a profound love for Campari.

It began when I was 18 and visited Venice for the first time. In every piazza there sat glamorous women in oversized sunglasses sipping a bright-red drink - a drink that glowed like a lantern

EIGHT

LA CUCINA

SARDA

LA CUCINA SARDA

Sardinian food does contain many of the same elements as that of mainland Italy. Artichokes, aubergines (eggplants) and tomatoes are the predominant vegetables; olive oil essential to cook and to season with; wine used liberally. Pasta is eaten daily and almost every dish contains some or other form of cheese. In *Italian Food*, Elizabeth David writes that the major fault of the Italian kitchen 'is the excessive use of cheese and the too frequent appearance of tomato sauce'. This accusation could certainly be levelled at Sardinia, but I personally have a boundless love for tomato sauce, and for cheese, and when both are well made, I don't think you can ever have an excessive amount of either. What David also highlights is the *freshness* of Italian food. Vegetables, fruit, meat and fish are bought in the morning and then cooked and eaten immediately. This also means there is very little waste, and whilst it might seem ludicrously extravagant and time-consuming, the produce is so cheap (because it is all grown here and needs no processing, refrigeration or preserving) that it makes sense economically, too.

The majority of the Sardinian diet is made up of vegetables, grains and pulses. Cheese is prolific, but other dairy products are rare: cream and butter are seldom used. Depending on budget, meat and fish are usually saved for special occasions, though special occasions seem to be frequent enough to be almost daily in Luca's family home.

Eating seasonally is not only *a* way of life for Sardinians; it is *the* way of life. Eating locally is not a novelty, but the norm. It is rare to find anything for sale that is not grown or produced in Italy, or more often on the island itself. Apart from bananas and broccoli there are no fruits or vegetables available perennially.

I have tried to adapt the recipes with an English kitchen in mind. Most of the ingredients are available in English supermarkets, or if not, can be found online or at Italian delis.

ARTICHOKES

The artichokes in Sardinia are some of the best in the world. For ways of eating them and cooking them, see page 61-64.

Almost every Sardinian home will preserve their own, and they are then cooked and preserved under oil to eat as an *antipasto* for the rest of the year. This process is laborious and can take all day, and friends will often come together to do it. The recipe for preserved artichokes is on page 66.

When choosing artichokes (in England or anywhere) try to buy them with their stalks attached. The stalks (if fresh) are good eaten too, when peeled right to the tender core. Choose those with a firm and tightly closed flower head - the tighter the better. These tend to be indicators of tenderness and sweetness. Also choose those with a long, pointed, tapered flower-head, rather than a fat squat one - another indication of tenderness.

BAY LEAVES

Bay is used prolifically in Sardinian cooking. I love its deep, herbal warmth, and appreciate the way it is often used as a final flavouring here, rather than simply as a base note. Many Sardinian dishes are finished with a generous handful of fresh bay leaves, which means the flavour stays bright and green and fights its way to the foreground.

BORAGE

Borage, an annual herb, grows wild all over the Mediterranean. I normally spy the first flowers by the roadside as early as February. Its violet-blue, star-shaped flowers are impossible to miss.

The flowers can be used to decorate soups, fish dishes and salads, or pastries and cakes. They have a mild, sweet, cucumber taste. The leaves, which are hairy and thick, are good coated in a light batter and deep fried, or used in the same way as nettles (blanched and chopped up in ravioli fillings or in soups).

Borage has been eaten and used in medicine throughout history. It is also associated with providing happiness and dispelling melancholy. According to Pliny the Elder, 'a decoction of borage takes away the sadness and gives joy to life', while John Gerard sites an old verse in *Gerard's Herball* that reads 'ego borago, gaudia semper ago', ('I borage, bring always courage').

A joy-bringer, and perhaps an early form of anti-depressant, borage has many things to offer the keen forager and gardener. The plant can be cultivated successfully in gardens in England and produces flowers in the summer. I grew up eating borage as my mother and grandmother always grew it, and put the flowers into Pimms.

BOTTARGA

A cured grey mullet roe known by chefs as 'the bacon of the sea,' bottarga is the most delicious food you've never heard of. I've written extensively about it on page 34.

CAPERS

Capers are another store-cupboard staple. If you have capers, anchovies and olives in jars in your store cupboard, all is well with the world, and you WILL be able to make something good to eat. Adding a delicious piquancy, they are blitzed into mayonnaise, tossed through salads and cooked slowly with meat; my favourite method is the last. Braised quail with capers is both utterly humble and delicious (page 172).

CHESTNUTS

Chestnuts grow all over Sardinia, and are a staple during the winter months. Most houses will have an open fire going all winter, over which they will roast chestnuts in a special pan, to be peeled and eaten with ash-black fingers. The nuts are nutrient rich, and are also used in soups and stews, as well as being milled into a delicious toasted flour.

FREGOLA/FREGULA

Fregola in Sardinia is cooked and treated more like rice than pasta, most often being cooked slowly in seafood dishes, broths and soups, until *al dente*. Occasionally it is boiled in lots of salted water like pasta and then seasoned afterwards. It is also delicious cold and in salads. It is a favourite for celebrations and weddings and goes particularly well with seafood.

LIMONCELLO

Limoncello, and *Mandarinetto*, are both common in Sardinia. Made from infusing alcohol with sugar and lemon or mandarin rind, it is a popular digestif. Also common is a *crema di Limone*, which is the same thing, but mixed with cream.

MIRTO

It is unlikely that you will leave Sardinia without having been offered *Mirto*. Made from infusing neat alcohol with the fragrant purple berries of the widespread wild myrtle bushes, it has a distinctive, herbal flavour and is usually drunk after meals.

MYRTLE

Myrtle grows wild all over Sardinia. The leaves have a slightly peppery, juniper and bay-like taste and are used for stuffing and perfuming roast meats, and for infusing poached fruit. The berries are used to infuse Sardinia's infamous liquor, *mirto*.

Myrtle is traditionally associated with Venus, goddess of 'love, beauty, pleasure and procreation,' which seems fitting, given that this is one of the pleasure-loving Sardinians' most beloved herbs.

ORANGES

Oranges have been grown in Italy since the 10th century, though they were originally used as flavourings and perfumes rather than eaten. In Italian history they evolved to be symbols of richness and opulence, so much so that the Medici family included them in their coat of arms. Oranges retain this sense of precious exoticism and provide a burst of colour and acidity in the darkest winter months. I'm not sure if I will ever grow tired of being able to pick my own oranges from a tree. In Sardinia, they are only available in their season, and are all grown locally. There are hundreds of varieties. In winter, I try to incorporate them into almost everything, both sweet and savoury.

PANCETTA AND GUANCIALE

Pancetta is an Italian bacon made from the belly of a pig which is cured with spices and salt. Guanciale is similar, but made from the cheek of the pig, so tends to have a gamier flavour and a higher fat content. Both are used widely in Sardinian soups and stews to add flavour and meaty depth. If you cannot find either, a good streaky bacon will do as a replacement.

PANE CARASAU

Pane carasau, or *carta di musica* (music-paper bread) is the most ancient and ubiquitous bread of Sardinia. The dough is made from semolina, salt and water, rolled into thin discs and cooked in a wood-fired oven until it puffs up. It is then split in half by hand into two even thinner discs, and baked again until completely crisp. It is deliciously moreish, and was designed to keep for many months at a time as a portable bread for Sardinian shepherds. The bread is still made by hand by many women in more rural areas.

PARSLEY

There are numerous theories that parsley originated in Sardinia, and whether these are true or not, its frequent use in the island's cuisine is indisputable.

Flat leaf parsley is cultivated here and used in almost every dish. It is also cooked at the beginning of many dishes, rather than just treated as a garnishing herb. Chopped parsley is often added with the *soffritto*, to provide a base flavouring for the sauce or stew. I have never come across this before, but it is very effective. When cooked in this way, it provides an earthy background not unlike celery (to which it is related).

PASTA

Dried pasta is eaten almost every day by most Sardinians. Fresh pasta is viewed as a treat and eaten only rarely. Franca has an entire double cupboard devoted to pasta, of every shape and variety (and by default, so do I). To check for quality, the best dried pasta should be made only from *semola di gran duro*. De Cecco is a trusted brand widely available in England. Pasta is covered in detail on page 114.

POLENTA

Polenta is a staple in my household. There are a few varieties available – those that cook slower, and 'quick-cook' strains. I use and like both. It is useful to always have a packet of polenta (cornmeal) on hand.

PURSLANE

Purslane is a type of succulent plant which has been eaten for centuries. The variety I find most often here has a thick crimson stem and small heart-shaped leaves. The leaves are juicy and mild-tasting and delicious in all salads.

RICE

Giuseppe, Luca's father, farms three different varieties on the family farm. These are a wild red rice known as Achilles, a black wild rice strain (originally from Asia) known as Venere (Venus) rice, and a white rice similar to carnaroli. These wild varieties cook slower and remain firmer to the bite, and have wonderfully aromatic flavours.

SAFFRON

Saffron is one of the signature flavours of Sardinian cuisine, and is grown around the region of Turri. Sardinia is now responsible for 60 per cent of Italy's overall saffron production. Another inheritance from the Phoenicians, saffron is used in both sweet and savoury cooking.

Cultivation is laborious (each crocus flower yields only three stigma) and therefore the spice is relatively expensive. Legend has it that saffron was once so prolific in Sardinia that it was used to give a yellow colour to malloreddus as it was cheaper than using eggs (page 122).

The flavour of saffron is a strange one. It is very strong, and should be used in small quantities otherwise it can overwhelm. It has a sort of hay-like perfume, and a slight honey-sweetness. Its exotic flavour works well with rich dishes, with ricotta in tarts, with custards and panna cottas and particularly with cheese or tomato dishes. It can be bought in threads or powdered. Try to buy the threads if you can find them.

SALT

Sardinia produces its own sea salt, which is usually finely ground and a little damp. I use this in all my cooking. Any sea salt is fine. Bear in mind that Sardinian food is *very* highly seasoned. People here eat lots of salt and still live forever, so please do not be afraid of salt.

SORREL

Deriving its name from 'sour' (*sur* in Old French), sorrel is loved by chefs all over the world for its clean, lemony flavour, which works beautifully in salads, with fish and even in desserts. It looks much like a dock leaf, but is a pure, vibrant green with arrow-shaped leaves with a lemony taste. It grows throughout the year over here, and I love to use it in recipes.

SUGAR

Plain, white sugar bears none of the stigma here that it does in England. Most Sardinians drink a good two spoons in their morning coffees. Darker sugars are used rarely, though I still love to use them in many baking recipes.

TINNED TUNA

Again, it is common to buy fresh tuna and preserve it under olive oil. Tinned tuna in Italy is also generally good quality, and an invaluable ingredient in the kitchen. Try to buy the best quality you can, under olive oil.

WILD FENNEL

This grows wild all over Europe and can easily be spotted at the beginning of spring. It grows up in long, thin feathers amongst other weeds in the hedgerow. If when picked you can smell an unmistakable anise scent, then it is fennel. Not to be confused with ferula (and I have done this), which is poisonous. Ferula is larger, fluffier, and smells of nothing. Wild fennel is a delicious addition to numerous Sardinian dishes, but if you cannot find it, you can use the fronds of a fennel bulb or a few fennel seeds.

WILD ASPARAGUS

Skinnier and more purple than its cultivated cousin, wild asparagus begins to appear at the beginning of the spring. It has a more pungent, concentrated flavour but also a stringier, tougher texture, so here it is cooked long and slow, to bring out the flavour and also to tenderise it.

ODDS AND SODS

As Sardinian cooking is essentially poor cooking, very little is wasted, whether it be animal or vegetable. Think again about the bits and bobs in your kitchen that are so often thrown away, overlooked or forgotten about.

BONES

Of any and every sort, to be boiled into the essential *brodo*.

FAT/SKIN OF PORK

If you are trimming a pork chop, loin or any cut, make sure to keep the fat and trim. Keep in the fridge or freezer, and when you fry onions at the beginning of braising pulses, add this fat to give flavour and richness to the finished dish.

PARMESAN AND PECORINO RINDS

Please never, ever throw away a cheese rind. It is a vessel of cheesy-flavoured deliciousness. Add it to simmering soups, stews, pulses and sauces. Fish out before serving. I always eat it at this point.

PRAWN HEADS AND SHELLS

If you are lucky enough to be buying whole prawns (shrimps) with shell and head still attached, make sure to boil up them up into a delicious sweet stock, which you can then use to flavour sauces and risottos.

Above: Nonna Giulia

Left: Nonna Eugenia

Right: Nonna Titia
with baby Luca

ACKNOWLEDGEMENTS

It is perhaps telling that I started writing the acknowledgments before I wrote the book.

'Only you, Letiiiizia, would write a book back to front' said Luca.

No one can 'own' a recipe, really, but taking the time to tell someone how to do something is an act of generosity, and this book owes much to the kindness of others.

I am grateful to so many people for so much.

Firstly to Giuseppe and Francesca Vacca. This book simply wouldn't exist if you hadn't shared with me your stories, your food and your time.

To Luca, for his brutally blunt criticism, and constant encouragement, without which I would never have got my arse into gear.

To Gianni Sabatini, Zio Cicco, Maura Falchi, Matteo and Pietro Lichieri and numerous friends in Oristano who have given me advice and recipes.

To Librid Oristano for the free wifi and delicious fregola.

To HH English Language Centre, for allowing me to work the most randomly flexible hours, to disappear for long periods of time and to still employ me.

To Gabriele Sanna, for translation help, for Moka, for Tiny-minding and for Sardinian stories and suffocated cauliflower.

To my family: my brothers and my parents, who have been there always to pick up the pieces.

To Emily Dobbs, who has always encouraged and helped me ever since we first met over the salads at Spring.

To Rose Ashby, friend and tolerant head-chef, for her honesty and friendship.

To every chef I have ever worked with or for, who has tolerated my mess, my impatience, and my inability to listen to (or follow) their rules.

To Stefano Vallebona, for Sardinian good humour and unbelievable salami.

To Domu Antiga and the Lai family, for their generosity and wisdom, for allowing me to use their beautiful location and eat their delicious food.

To Kajal Mistry, for being the most positive editor anyone could wish for. To Eve Marleau for her reassurance and editing prowess.

To Anne Kibel, my agent, for taking a chance.

To my grandmother who taught me to love food in the first place, and who I wish had lived to see this book.

To Nonna Giulia, the feistiest Nonna in town.

To Vicky Green for help with editing, and much appreciated visits.

To Harriet Piercy for grammatical corrections and help.

To Yossy Arefi, for introducing me to olive oil ice cream.

To Claudia Casu for teaching me the method for culurgionis.

To Matt Russell for his beautiful photographs and for being a 'magician with light'.

To Maria Bell, for her stunning photographs.

To Tamara Vos for her wonderful styling, and Louie Waller for her fantastic props. To Olivia Williamson for assisting and beautiful photographs.

To Evi-O Studio for the stunning design and illustrations.

And to everyone else who has contributed in some way which I cannot currently think of. *Grazie!*

Left: Giuseppe (left) and his brother Paolo

Right: Franca (Luca's mum)

ABOUT THE AUTHOR

Letitia Clark is a food writer, illustrator and chef. Born in Devon, Letitia gained a degree and Masters in English Literature before deciding to pursue her other passion, food, and to train as a chef. She completed the Leiths diploma in Food and Wine and went on to work in some of London's top restaurants, including Spring, Morito and The Dock Kitchen. In 2017 she moved from East London to Sardinia, and began writing about food, as well as painting and illustrating.

letitiaclark.co.uk

INDEX

INDEX

T

V

W

Y

Z

IMPRINT

Published in 2020 by Hardie Grant Books,
an imprint of Hardie Grant Publishing

Hardie Grant Books (London)
5th & 6th Floors
52-54 Southwark Street
London, SE1 1UN

Hardie Grant Books (Melbourne)
Building 1, 658 Church Street
Richmond, Victoria 3121

hardiegrantbooks.com

British Library Cataloguing-in-Publication Data.
A catalogue record for this book is available
from the British Library.

Bitter Honey by Letitia Clark

ISBN: 978-1-78488-277-8

Publishing Director: Kate Pollard
Commissioning Editor: Kajal Mistry
Senior Editor: Eve Marleau
Designer: Evi-O.Studio | Susan Le
Design Assistants: Evi-O.Studio | Karina Camenzind
Photographers: Matt Russell, Maria Bell
Photography Assistant: Matthew Hague
Food Stylist: Tamara Vos
Food Styling Assistant: Olivia Williamson
Prop Stylist: Louie Waller
Editor: Eve Marleau
Proofreader: Taahir Husain
Indexer: Vanessa Bird

Colour reproduction by p2d
Printed and bound in China by Leo Paper Products Ltd.